Kerry Bretherton QC is a silk who specialises in property, property development and related commercial transactions. She deals with all aspects of development work, real property and commercial and residential landlord and tenant for a variety of clients including developers, companies and private individuals. Kerry also deals with public law cases which are related to property work, with experience on the AG A Panel prior to her appointment to silk, and her clients include central and local government. Kerry has regularly appeared in the Court of Appeal and Supreme Court and has been counsel in some of the leading property cases. Kerry is ranked in Chambers & Partners 2021 and Legal 500.

James Castle is a junior barrister at Tanfield Chambers who specialises in property litigation. This includes real property disputes, the law of landlord and tenant (both commercial and residential), and of course the Electronic Communications Code. And because property cases often involve other elements, James also regularly deals with commercial debts, insolvency issues, company law and even harassment.

A Practical Guide to the New Electronic Communications Code for Property Lawyers

A Practical Guide to the New Electronic Communications Code for Property Lawyers

Kerry Bretherton QC
Barrister, Tanfield Chambers
BA (Hons)

James Castle
Barrister, Tanfield Chambers
BA (Hons) (Oxon)

Law Brief Publishing

Published 2022 by Law Brief Publishing, an imprint of Law Brief Publishing Ltd
30 The Parks
Minehead
Somerset
TA24 8BT

www.lawbriefpublishing.com

Paperback: 978-1-914608-09-4

For our grandfathers:

Fred Wakeling (Kerry's grandad) and
Leslie Castle (James's grandpa),
without whom this book would never have been written

We owe our careers at the Bar to each of you

PREFACE

We have written this book on the new Electronic Communications Code ("**the Code**") to serve both as a first port of call for practitioners new to the regime, and as a useful reference point for those familiar with the regime.

Our focus has been primarily on those parts of the Code that are most likely to come up in practice, rather than on creating a comprehensive guide to every aspect of the Code. But this does not mean that this will be a purely whistle-stop tour. Due consideration is given to the various complexities of the new regime, especially in the context of the substantial consideration of the Code by the courts since it came into force (and the Code is due to be considered for the first time by the Supreme Court in 2022).

We outline the parts of the Code that fall within the scope of this book and those that do not in Chapter 1: An Introduction to the New Electronic Communications Code. This first chapter also contains a section on the Operation and Content of the Code and this Book.

It should be noted that whilst parts of the Code do apply to other jurisdictions, this book only deals with how it applies in England and Wales.

The law is correct as at 1 December 2021.

Kerry Bretherton QC
Barrister, Tanfield Chambers

James Castle
Barrister, Tanfield Chambers

December 2021

CONTENTS

TABLE OF CASES

TABLE OF STATUTES

TABLE OF STATUTORY INSTRUMENTS

CHAPTER ONE

AN INTRODUCTION TO THE NEW ELECTRONIC COMMUNICATIONS CODE

This introductory chapter deals with the following topics:

(1) The development of the new Electronic Communications Code ("**the Code**")[1] to replace the old Electronic Communications Code ("**the Old Code**");[2]

(2) The purpose of the Code; and

(3) An overview of how the Code operates, and its contents.

The Development of the Code

Electronic communications ("**telecoms**") infrastructure is the beating heart of modern society in our digital age. This has never been truer than in the wake of the Coronavirus pandemic, which has prompted developed countries across the world to adapt to socially distanced life by embracing new remote means of communication. The United Kingdom's telecoms apparatus is now relied upon heavily not just in our homes and businesses, but also by HM Courts & Tribunals Service, the National Health Service and even our schools.

The technology involved in maintaining these services develops at an alarming rate; as a result, electronic data transmission rates have been growing exponentially for decades. This is one of the reasons why the

[1] The Code can be found set out as Schedule 3A of the Communications Act 2003, and was inserted there by Section 4(2) and Schedule 1 of the Digital Economy Act 2017.

[2] The Old Code was contained at Schedule 2 to the Telecommunications Act 1984, but is now repealed.

statutory regime governing the relationships in the United Kingdom between its telecoms network operators and the landowners on whose land they erect their telecoms apparatus ought to be regularly reviewed and updated.

But until 28 December 2017, the United Kingdom was still using its original telecoms code, the Old Code set out in Schedule 2 to the Telecommunications Act 1984. A code, drafted before the invention of the World Wide Web, that it was envisaged would regulate the rollout of landline telephones across the United Kingdom.[3] Its draftsmen could barely have conceived of fibre-optic broadband or the 5G mobile network.

However, when the Law Commission published its independent review of the Old Code on 28 February 2013, its reasons for recommending reform were not limited to simply future proofing the existing statutory regime against emerging technologies.[4] The Law Commission recognised that the Old Code has been condemned judicially as *"not one of Parliament's better drafting efforts... one of the least coherent and thought-through pieces of legislation on the statute book"*,[5] and recommended extensive reforms to (inexhaustively):

(1) Clarify the valuation principles for determining the consideration that landowners can charge telecoms network operators for the use of their land to host telecoms apparatus;

(2) Resolve inconsistencies between the Old Code and other legislation, such as the Land Registration Act 2002 and the Landlord and Tenant Act 1954;

[3] Albeit that it was substantially amended with effect from 25 July 2003 by Schedule 3 of the Communications Act 2003 to (1) comply with five Directives issued by the European Union and (2) reflect some developments in technology.

[4] The Law Commission, *The Electronic Communications Code* (LAW COM No 336).

[5] *Geo Networks Ltd v The Bridgewater Canal Company Ltd* [2010] 1 WLR 2576 at [7], by Lewison J (as he then was).

(3) Clarify which third parties ought to be bound by rights conferred on telecoms network operators by landowners;

(4) Improve the procedure for resolving disputes arising under the Old Code;

(5) Clarify the process for terminating agreements falling under the Old Code; and

(6) Give limited new rights to telecoms network operators to upgrade and share their network equipment, given the emergence of new technologies that could enable telecoms network operators to save costs with the benefit of these new rights (passing those costs savings onto consumers).

In December 2014, HM Government's Department for Culture, Media and Sport (the Department for Digital, Culture, Media and Sport since 3 July 2017 – our emphasis) announced that it would reform the Old Code based on the Law Commission's recommendations. It consulted on its draft legislation between February and April 2015,[6] and published its revised proposals for a new code on 17 May 2016.[7]

HM Government's proposed reforms largely aligned with the Law Commission's original recommendations. This included the recommendation that any new code does not have retrospective effect, but instead provides for the Old Code to become 'naturally' obsolete as agreements subject to the Old Code are either terminated or renewed under the new regime.

However, following independent economic analysis, HM Government did decide to adopt a new (and controversial) basis for the valuation of rights conferred under agreements falling within the remit of the new statutory regime. Whereas the Old Code valued rights on an open market

---

[6] Department for Culture, Media and Sport, *Reforming the Electronic Communications Code: Consultation Document*, 26 February 2015.

[7] Department for Culture, Media and Sport, *A New Electronic Communications Code*, May 2016.

basis, the Code values them on a 'no scheme' basis, dramatically altering the potential value of the rights.

The end result was the coming into force of the Code on 27 December 2017.[8]

The Purpose of the Code

We have set out above that the Code is designed to regulate contractual relationships between telecoms network operators and landowners. But the Code itself does not clearly state why it exists; what purpose the regulation serves.

Assistance can instead be drawn from Law Commission's review of the Old Code. It says that a telecoms code needs to exist to (again, inexhaustively):

(1) Ensure that the availability of telecoms services are not impeded by telecoms operators having difficulties gaining access to land;

(2) Strike a fair balance between the rights of landowners and the public interest in the provision of telecoms services across the United Kingdom; and

(3) Make certain the legal consequences of agreements between telecoms operators and landowners on third parties.[9]

---

[8] The Code is yet to be substantially amended, but – following a consultation that ran from 27 January 2021 to 24 March 2021 – in respect of (1) obtaining and using code agreements (2) rights to upgrade and share apparatus and (3) expired agreements – it appears that HM Government has plans to make amendments to the Code. Those plans are presently contained in Part 2 of the Product Security and Telecommunications Bill, which was introduced in the House of Commons on 24 November 2021.

[9] See Department for Culture, Media and Sport, *Reforming the Electronic Communications Code: Consultation Document*, 26 February 2015, Paragraphs 2.3 to 2.11 for a full digest of the Law Commission's views on the purpose of a telecoms code.

In the following chapters, we will set out the various ways in which these envisioned purposes indeed ring true in the Code. In particular, the reader will see that the issue of whether a fair balance is struck between the public interest and the rights of landowners is central to both the extent of the court's power to impose code agreement terms on parties, and the new valuation basis for code agreements.

The Operation and Content of the Code and this Book

The Code creates a scheme whereby relevant telecoms operators can serve notice on landowners indicating a desire to acquire rights over their land for the purpose of furthering their telecoms networks. If the parties reach agreement on the terms of acquisition of those rights, then a qualifying agreement under the Code ("**code agreement**") is created. If the parties are in dispute, the courts will adjudicate (in an expedited timeframe) and impose a code agreement if relevant criteria are met.

The core parts of the Code that are dealt with in this book are as follows:

(1) Part 1 of the Code, entitled 'Key Concepts' [10] sets out the various definitions that form the foundation for the Code. It deals with who the relevant telecoms operators are, what qualifies as telecoms apparatus and a telecoms network, and what core rights telecoms operators can seek to acquire under the Code ("**code rights**"). These matters are considered in more detail in Chapter 2;

(2) Part 2 of the Code, entitled 'Conferral of Code Rights and their Exercise' [11] is eclectic. It deals with the circumstances under which code rights can be exercised and the relevant persons who can be compelled to enter into code agreements (Chapter 3), and the third parties that may be bound by code agreements (Chapters 3 and 11);

(3) Part 3 of the Code, entitled 'Assignment of Code Rights, and Upgrading and Sharing of Apparatus' [12] is self-explanatory. The

---

[10] Communications Act 2003, Schedule 3A, Paragraphs 1 to 7.

[11] Ibid, Paragraphs 8 to 14.

[12] Ibid, Paragraphs 15 to 18.

'bonus rights' to upgrade and share telecoms apparatus are explored in Chapter 2, and assignment is considered in Chapter 11;

(4) Part 4 of the Code, entitled 'Power of the Court to Impose Agreement' [13] is far-reaching. It provides the power of the court to impose code agreement terms (Chapter 4), the formalities for code agreements and the kind of terms that can be included within code agreements (Chapter 5) and the new valuation basis (Chapter 6);

(5) Part 5 of the Code, entitled 'Termination and Modification of Agreements' [14] also contains the provisions for continuation and novation of code agreements. Continuation and termination are considered in Chapter 8, whereas modification and novation are found in Chapter 9;

(6) Part 6 of the Code, entitled 'Right to Require Removal of Electronic Communications Apparatus' [15] is dealt with in Chapter 10; and

(7) In addition, this book contains chapters on landowners' rights to compensation payable under the Code (Chapter 7), the transitional provisions bridging the Old Code and the Code (Chapter 12) and on alternative dispute resolution, and the procedures and practicalities of litigating under the Code (Chapter 13).

This book does not pretend to comprehensively discuss every aspect of the Code. In particular, Part 4A of the Code [16] (which is not yet in force) and Parts 7 to 12 of the Code [17] lie outside the scope of this book. As does detailed consideration of the workings of the Old Code.

---

[13] Ibid, Paragraphs 19 to 27.

[14] Ibid, Paragraphs 28 to 35.

[15] Ibid, Paragraphs 36 to 44.

[16] Entitled 'Code Rights in Respect of Lad Connected to Leased Premises: Unresponsive Occupiers'.

[17] Which deal with: conferral of transport land rights and their exercise; conferral of street work rights and their exercise; conferral of tidal water rights and their exercise; undertaker's works affecting electronic communications apparatus; overhead

Summary

In summary:

(1) The Code was not brought in simply because the Old Code was not up to the task of keeping up with developing technologies. The Old Code had a number of serious flaws, including poor drafting, and required extensive reform to operate satisfactorily both in the modern day and in the context of other statutory regimes;

(2) The Code regulates the contractual relationships between telecoms operators and landowners chiefly to ensure that the former has sufficient access to the land it needs to provide services that are in the public interest, and also to ensure that third parties can be certain where they stand in respect of those agreements; and

(3) The Code operates by giving telecoms operators the power to compel landowners to enter into agreements with them for the conferral of code rights. Provided the relevant formalities are complied with, in default of agreement the courts will adjudicate the dispute and may impose a code agreement and decide its terms, including the payment of consideration and compensation. The Code also provides for the circumstances under which code agreements may be terminated (after which, when and how telecoms apparatus must be removed from the subject land) or varied.

---

apparatus; and rights to object to certain apparatus installed on, over or under tidal water or lands.

CHAPTER TWO

CODE OPERATORS, THEIR NETWORKS, AND CODE RIGHTS

This chapter explores the following:

(1) Which telecoms network operators are subject to the Code;

(2) What qualifies as telecoms apparatus and telecoms networks;

(3) The code rights and their exercise; and

(4) The power for telecoms network operators to upgrade or share their telecoms apparatus.

Code Operators

The Code is designed to regulate contractual relationships between landowners and certain telecoms network operators concerning rights granted in respect of telecoms apparatus. The relevant telecoms network operators are identified in Section 106 of the Communications Act 2003 ("**the 2003 Act**"):

"(3) The electronic communications code shall have effect—

(a) in the case of a person to whom it is applied by a direction given by OFCOM; and

(b) in the case of the Secretary of State or any Northern Ireland department where the Secretary of State or that department is providing or proposing to provide an electronic communications network.

(4) The only purposes for which the electronic communications code may be applied in a person's case by a direction under this section are—

(a) the purposes of the provision by him of an electronic communications network; or

(b) the purposes by him of a system of infrastructure which he is making available, or proposing to make available, for use by providers of electronic communications networks for the purposes of the provision by them of their networks.

(5) A direction applying the electronic communications code in any person's case may provide for that code to have effect in his case—

(a) in relation only to such places or localities as may be specified or described in the direction;

(b) for the purposes only of the provision of such electronic communications network, or part of an electronic communications network, as may be so specified or described; or

(c) for the purposes only of the provision of such system of infrastructure, or part of a system of infrastructure, as may be so specified or described." [1]

Pursuant to Section 108(1) of the 2003 Act, the Office of Communications ("**OFCOM**") keeps a register of all persons to whom the Code applies by virtue of a directive under Section 106.[2] At present, there are over 200 telecoms network operators on OFCOM's register ("**code operators**").

Telecoms Apparatus and Networks

What qualifies as telecoms apparatus is set out in Paragraph 5 of the Code:

"(1) In this code "electronic communications apparatus" means—

---

[1] Communications Act 2003, Section 106(3) to (5).

[2] The register can be found at https://www.ofcom.org.uk/phones-telecoms-and-internet/information-for-industry/policy/electronic-comm-code/register-of-persons-with-powers-under-the-electronic-communications-code.

> *(a) apparatus designed or adapted for use in connection with the provision of an electronic communications network,*
>
> *(b) apparatus designed or adapted for a use which consists of or includes the sending or receiving of communications or other signals that are transmitted by means of an electronic communications network,*
>
> *(c) lines, and*
>
> *(d) other structures or things designed or adapted for use in connection with the provision of an electronic communications network...*
>
> *(3) In this code—*
>
> *"line" means any wire, cable, tube, pipe or similar thing (including its casing or coating) which is designed or adapted for use in connection with the provision of any electronic communications network or electronic communications service;*
>
> *"structure" includes a building only if the sole purpose of that building is to enclose other electronic communications apparatus."*[3]

The definition contains no reference to any specific type of equipment or to any kind of telecoms service that said equipment might facilitate. This wording was chosen carefully, upon a recommendation contained in the Law Commission's review of the Old Code, to ensure that the description of telecoms apparatus is 'technologically neutral'.[4] The goal being to ensure that, as telecoms technology evolves to the point that it no longer resembles existing technologies, the court does not find itself adjudicating disputes between telecoms operators and landowners about whether or not new telecoms equipment actually falls within the remit of the Code.

---

3 Communications Act 2003, Schedule 3A, Paragraph 5(1) and (3).

4 Department for Culture, Media and Sport, *Reforming the Electronic Communications Code: Consultation Document*, 26 February 2015, Paragraph 1.28.

The definition of telecoms networks, contained in Paragraphs 6 and 7 of the Code, is given similar treatment, in order to have as broad a definition as possible. Paragraph 6 reads:

"In this code "network" in relation to an operator means—

(a) if the operator falls within paragraph 2(a), so much of any electronic communications network or infrastructure system provided by the operator as is not excluded from the application of the code under section 106(5), and

(b) if the operator falls within paragraph 2(b), the electronic communications network which the Secretary of State or the Northern Ireland department is providing or proposing to provide."[5]

And Paragraph 7 of the Code provides for a similarly wide definition of *"infrastructure system"*:

"(1) In this code "infrastructure system" means a system of infrastructure provided so as to be available for use by providers of electronic communications networks for the purposes of the provision by them of their networks.

(2) References in this code to provision of an infrastructure system include references to establishing or maintaining such a system."

Code Rights and their Exercise

Paragraph 3 of the Code sets out the nine core rights that telecoms operators can seek to acquire from landowners under a code agreement:

"For the purposes of this code a "code right", in relation to an operator and any land, is a right for the statutory purposes—

(a) to install electronic communications apparatus on, under or over the land,

[5] Communications Act 2003, Schedule 3A, Paragraph 6.

(b) to keep installed electronic communications apparatus which is on, under or over the land,

(c) to inspect, maintain, adjust, alter, repair, upgrade or operate electronic communications apparatus which is on, under or over the land,

(d) to carry out any works on the land for or in connection with the installation of electronic communications apparatus on, under or over the land or elsewhere,[6]

(e) to carry out any works on the land for or in connection with the maintenance, adjustment, alteration, repair, upgrading or operation of electronic communications apparatus which is on, under or over the land or elsewhere,

(f) to enter the land to inspect, maintain, adjust, alter, repair, upgrade or operate any electronic communications apparatus which is on, under or over the land or elsewhere,

(g) to connect to a power supply,

(h) to interfere with or obstruct a means of access to or from the land (whether or not any electronic communications apparatus is on, under or over the land), or

(i) to lop or cut back, or require another person to lop or cut back, any tree or other vegetation that interferes or will or may interfere with electronic communications apparatus."[7]

And the definition of *"the statutory purposes"* is set out in Paragraph 4 of the Code:

"(a) the purposes of providing the operator's network, or

---

[6] In *EE Ltd v MacDonald* [2020] 3 WLUK 511 the Lands Tribunal (Scotland) held that Paragraph 3(d) of the Code should be interpreted widely enough (and purposively) so as to be capable of giving a code operator an express right to take access over land in order to install telecoms apparatus on other land.

[7] Ibid, Paragraph 3.

(b) the purposes of providing an infrastructure system."[8]

Most of these rights broadly mirror those that were available under the Old Code.[9] But some of the rights contained at Paragraph 3(f), (g), (h) and (i) of the Code are either completely (or mostly) new:

(1) Under Paragraph 3(f) and (h), code operators can now acquire the right to access (or the right to obstruct access to) land neighbouring the land where they have installed their telecoms apparatus;

(2) Under Paragraph 3(g), code operators can now acquire the right to connect their telecoms apparatus to a local power supply, paid for by the landowner. Any electricity used by the telecoms operator that is paid for by the landowner is likely to be reflected in the compensation payable by the telecoms operator to the landowner; and

(3) Under Paragraph 3(i), what previously existed only as a power to give notice to an occupier of land to cut back a tree growing on their land has been turned into a code right that extends to all vegetation, not just to trees, [10] and allows the telecoms operator to choose between doing the work itself or requiring another to do it.[11]

Code rights, once acquired under a code agreement, can only be exercised in accordance with *"the terms subject to which it is conferred"* [12] and anything done by a code operator *"in the exercise of a code right conferred*

---

[8] Ibid, Paragraph 4.

[9] See Telecommunications Act 1984, Schedule 2, Paragraph 2(1).

[10] Ibid, Paragraph 19.

[11] The old power to give notice to achieve similar as been retained and updated in Paragraph 82 of the Code. Under that provision, code operators may serve a notice on an occupier of land requiring them to lop back a tree or vegetation that may obstruct or interfere with their telecoms apparatus regardless of whether this has been conferred on the code operator by that person as a code right under a code agreement. There is then provision for a counter-notice to be served, and for the court to determine whether the code operator's notice takes effect (if not already complied with) and whether to award compensation. For notices generally, see Chapter 3.

[12] Communications Act 2003, Schedule 3A, Paragraph 12(1).

under this Part in relation to any land is to be treated as done in the exercise of a statutory power."[13]

The Power to Upgrade or Share Telecoms Apparatus

Also new are the two bonus rights to upgrade and share telecoms apparatus that are automatically conferred on all telecoms operators who enter into code agreements under Part 2 of the Code.[14] These bonus rights are subject to two conditions, as set out in Paragraph 17 of the Code:

"(1) An operator ("the main operator") who has entered into an agreement under Part 2 of this code may, if the conditions in sub-paragraphs (2) and (3) are met—

(a) upgrade the electronic communications apparatus to which the agreement relates, or

(b) share the use of such electronic communications apparatus with another operator.

(2) *The first condition is that any changes as a result of the upgrading or sharing to the electronic communications apparatus to which the agreement relates have no adverse impact, or no more than a minimal adverse impact, on its appearance.*

(3) The second condition is that the upgrading or sharing imposes no additional burden on the other party to the agreement.

(4) For the purposes of sub-paragraph (3) an additional burden includes anything that—

[13] Ibid, Paragraph 12(2).

[14] Save where the exercise of the code right conferred under the code agreement depends on a right that has effect pursuant to an agreement that was entered into under the Old Code. See Chapter 12 and Digital Economy Act 2017, Schedule 2, Paragraph 5(2).

(a) has an additional adverse effect on the other party's enjoyment of the land, or

(b) causes additional loss, damage or expense to that party." [15]

Further, pursuant to Paragraph 17(5) of the Code, it is not possible to contract out of these bonus rights being conferred on the telecoms operator by the landowner. Nor is it possible to agree to make use of the 'bonus rights' subject to any conditions *"including a condition requiring the payment of money"*.[16]

The interpretation of Paragraph 17 of the Code was one of the matters in dispute in *Cornerstone Telecommunications Infrastructure Ltd v London and Quadrant Housing Trust*.[17] The dispute concerned the terms on which rights ought to have been imposed by the court under the Code over a new telecoms site on the roof of a large block of flats.

At [64] of his judgment, Martin Roger QC highlighted that the right to upgrade and share telecoms apparatus are not treated the same under the Code: the former is *both* a code right and a bonus right under Paragraph 17; the latter is solely a bonus right.

When considering the two conditions at Paragraphs 17(2) and (3) of the Code, Martin Roger QC came to the following conclusions:

(1) The reference in Paragraph 17(2) to whether changes to the telecoms apparatus has *"no adverse impact, or no more than a minimal adverse impact, on its appearance"* refers to the appearance of the telecoms apparatus itself, not to the land or building on which it has been erected;[18]

(2) Unlike in Paragraph 17(2), Paragraph 17(3) has no *de minimis* exception. So, the 'bonus right' to share or upgrade in Paragraph 17

[15] Communications Act 2003, Schedule 3A, Paragraph 17(1) to (4).

[16] Ibid, Paragraph 17(5).

[17] [2020] UKUT 282 (LC).

[18] Ibid, [73].

cannot be exercised under any circumstances if doing so would impose any additional burden at all on the landowner subject to the code agreement;[19]

(3) As a result, Paragraph 17's 'bonus rights' are an *"irreducible minimum"* to which code operators are entitled to as of right under the Code.

(4) Given that the right to upgrade is a code right, it is open to a code operator to seek a code right to upgrade that would exceed the right it is entitled to already under Paragraph 17, but this would have to meet the relevant criteria for the imposition of any other code right to the extent that the right sought exceeded the Paragraph 17 entitlement.[20]

As the right to share telecoms apparatus with other telecoms operators is not a code right, it appears that it would not be possible for a code operator to seek the imposition of a right to share in excess of the right conferred under Paragraph 17.

Summary

In summary:

(1) The Code only applies to those telecoms operators who have received a directive from OFCOM, and are contained in OFCOM's official register (and Secretaries of State);

(2) Both telecoms equipment and telecoms networks have been 'technologically neutral' definitions to future-proof the Code against the development of new telecoms technologies and systems;

(3) We have set out the code rights themselves, and how they broadly mirror the rights under the Old Code save for new rights to connect to a power supply, access and obstruct access to neighbouring land,

---

19 Ibid, [73].

20 Ibid, [77].

and lop or cut back any vegetation that may interfere with telecoms equipment; and

(4) Bonus rights to share and upgrade telecoms apparatus are conferred automatically with all code agreements, but these rights are an *"irreducible minimum"* that can only be exercised if two conditions are met. It is possible for telecoms operators to seek a code right to upgrade not subject to those conditions, but not to share as sharing telecoms apparatus with other telecoms operators is not a code right in and of itself.

CHAPTER THREE

NOTICES, THEIR SERVICE, AND PARAGRAPH 20 NOTICES

This chapter deals with the following topics:

(1) The general requirements for all forms of notice given under the Code;

(2) Service of notices given under the Code;

(3) How code operators commence the process of entering code agreements by serving a notice pursuant to Paragraph 20 of the Code ("**Paragraph 20 notice**"); and

(4) The identity of the *"relevant person"* upon whom the Paragraph 20 notice should be served.

The General Requirements for Notices Given Under the Code

Part 15 of the Code contains the provisions in respect of notices given under the Code generally.

Notices Given by Code Operators

Paragraph 88 of the Code sets out the requirements for all notices given by code operators. Such notices must:

"(a) explain the effect of the notice,

(b) explain which provisions of this code are relevant to the notice, and

(c) explain the steps that may be taken by the recipient in respect of the notice."[1]

As set out above, OFCOM are obliged by Paragraph 90(1) of the Code to prescribe all forms of notice that can be given under the Code, and have done so. OFCOM's prescribed form of notices must be used by code operators.[2]

Failure to comply with the requirements of Paragraph 88 of the Code renders any notice given by a code operator invalid,[3] unless the person receiving the notice chooses to rely on the notice and treat it as valid.[4]

Notices Given by Others

Pursuant to Paragraphs 89(1) to (4) of the Code:

(1) OFCOM's prescribed form of notice to be given under Paragraphs 31(1) (termination notices)[5] 33(1) (variation notices),[6] 39(1) and 40(2) (notices relating to the identification and removal of telecoms apparatus)[7] of the Code must be used by persons other than code operators;[8] and

(2) Failure to do so renders any notice given invalid, unless the code operator chooses to rely upon the notice received and treat it as valid.[9]

---

[1] Communications Act 2003, Schedule 3A, Paragraph 88(1).

[2] Ibid, Paragraph 88(2). And a certificate issued by OFCOM stating that a particular form of notice used by a code operator has been prescribed by them is conclusive evidence of that fact, pursuant to Paragraph 88(5).

[3] Ibid, Paragraph 88(3).

[4] Ibid, Paragraph 88(4).

[5] For which, see Chapter 8.

[6] For which, see Chapter 9.

[7] For which, see Chapter 10.

[8] Communications Act 2003, Schedule 3A, Paragraphs 89(1) and (2). And a certificate issued by OFCOM stating that a particular form of notice used by a person other than a code operator has been prescribed by them is conclusive evidence of that fact, pursuant to Paragraph 89(7).

[9] Ibid, Paragraphs 89(3) and (4).

Where:

(1) A notice is given by a code operator to an other person ("**the Operator's Notice**"),

(2) The other person gives a notice in response to the Operator's Notice ("**the Responding Notice**") (e.g. a relevant counter-notice),

(3) OFCOM have prescribed the form of Responding Notice, and

(4) The operator, when giving the Operator's Notice, drew the other person's attention to the prescribed form of Responding Notice – [10]

the Operator's Notice is a valid notice for the purposes of the Code regardless, but if the other person has failed to use the form prescribed by OFCOM then *"the person giving the notice must bear any costs incurred by the operator as a result of the notice not being in that form"*.[11]

It follows that where the code operator fails, when giving the Operator's Notice, to draw the other person's attention to the prescribed form of Responding Notice then a failure to use that prescribed form by the other person:

(1) Does not render the Responding Notice invalid; and

(2) The other person will not be liable to bear the code operator's costs incurred as a result of the Responding Notice not being in the prescribed form.

The Service of Notices Given Under the Code

Service of notices given under the Code is dealt with at Paragraph 91:

"(1) A notice given under this code must not be sent by post unless it is sent by a registered post service or by recorded delivery.

(2) For the purposes, in the case of a notice under this code, of section 394 of this Act (service of notifications and other documents) and section 7 of

[10] Communications Act 2003, Schedule 3A, Paragraph 89(5).

[11] Ibid, Paragraph 89(6).

the Interpretation Act 1978 (references to service by post), the proper address of a person ("P") is–

(a) if P has given the person giving the notice an address for service under this code that address, and

(b) otherwise, the address given by section 394."[12]

Section 394 of the 2003 Act sets out that notices required to be sent under the Code may be delivered to the relevant person, left at their *"proper address"* or be sent by post to their *"proper address"*.[13] Further, that:

"(4) The notification or document may be given or sent to a body corporate by being given or sent to the secretary or clerk of that body.

(5) The notification or document may be given or sent to a firm by being given or sent to–

(a) a partner in the firm; or

(b) a person having the control or management of the partnership business."

(6) The notification or document may be given or sent to an unincorporated body or association by being given or sent to a member of the governing body of the body or association.

(7) For the purposes of this section and section 7 of the Interpretation Act 1978 (c. 30) (service of documents by post) in its application to this section, the proper address of that person is–

(a) in the case of body corporate, the address of the registered or principal office of the body;

(b) in the case of a firm, unincorporated body or association, the address of the principal office of the partnership, body or association;

---

[12] Ibid, Paragraph 91(1) and (2).

[13] Communications Act 2003, Section 394(3).

(c) in the case of a person to whom the notification or other document is given or sent in reliance on any of subsections (4) to (6), the proper address of the body corporate, firm or (as the case may be) other body or association in question; and

(d) in any other case, the last known address of the person in question." [14]

And for companies registered outside the United Kingdom, firms carrying on business outside the United Kingdom, or unincorporated bodies or associations with offices outside the United Kingdom, references in Section 394(7) of the 2003 Act to *"its principal office includes references to its principal office within the United Kingdom (if any)."* [15]

Section 394 of the 2003 Act is expressly subject to Section 395, which provides for service by electronic means making use of a telecoms network.[16] Section 395 of the 2003 Act provides that (for example) e-mail service of a notice *"has effect for the purposes of the enactments specified in section 394(2) as a delivery of the notification or other document to the recipient, but only if the requirements imposed by or under this section are complied with."* [17]

There are then different requirements depending on whom the notice is to be served. Provided that the intended recipient is not OFCOM itself, the recipient (or any agent of the recipient) *"must have indicated to the person making the transmission the recipient's willingness to receive notifications or documents transmitted in the form and manner used."* [18] Such an indication:

"(a) must be given to [the person making the transmission] *in such manner as he may require;*

---

[14] Ibid, Section 394(4) to (7).

[15] Ibid, Section 394(8).

[16] Ibid, Section 394(10).

[17] Ibid, Section 395(2).

[18] Ibid, Section 395(5). For notices served on OFCOM, see Section 395(3) and (4).

(b) may be a general indication or one that is limited to notifications or documents of a particular description;

(c) must state the address to be used and must be accompanied by such other information as that person requires for the making of the transmission; and

(d) may be modified or withdrawn at any time by a notice given to that person in such manner as he may require." [19]

So, notices given under the Code can be delivered to the recipient, delivered to their *"proper address"*, or posted to them at their *"proper address"* (provided that the notice is sent by registered post or recorded delivery). Provided that willingness to receive a notice by electronic means has been given by the recipient to the transmitter, service by (for example) e-mail is permitted and takes effect as a delivery to the recipient.

Paragraph 91 goes on, however, to explain how service of a relevant notice may be effected in the event that it is not possible to find out after *"reasonable enquiries the name and address of a person who is"* either the *"occupier of land for the purposes of this code"* or *"the owner of an interest in land."* [20] In respect of the former –

"(4) A notice may be given under this code to the occupier —

(a) by addressing it to a person by the description of "occupier" of the land (and describing the land), and

(b) by delivering it to a person who is on the land or, if there is no person on the land to whom it can be delivered, by affixing it, or a copy of it, to a conspicuous object on the land" [21] –

and of the latter –

[19] Ibid, Section 395(6).

[20] Ibid, Schedule 3A, Paragraph 91(3) and (5).

[21] Ibid, Paragraph 91(4).

"(6) A notice may be given under this code to the owner—

(a) by addressing it to a person by the description of "owner" of the interest (and describing the interest and the land), and

(b) by delivering it to a person who is on the land or, if there is no person on the land to whom it can be delivered, by affixing it, or a copy of it, to a conspicuous object on the land." [22]

Paragraph 20 Notices

One of the most important notices that can be given under the Code is the Paragraph 20 notice, which is given by a code operator when it has identified a piece of land over which it has decided to acquire one or more code rights in order to improve its telecoms network. Rather than simply approaching the landowner and seeking to negotiate terms, the code operator must serve a Paragraph 20 notice. Paragraph 20 of the Code provides that:

"(1) … where the operator requires a person (a "relevant person") to agree—

(a) to confer a code right on the operator, or

(b) to be otherwise bound by a code right which is exercisable by the operator.

(2) The operator may give the relevant person a notice in writing—

(a) setting out the code right, and all of the other terms of the agreement that the operator seeks, and

(b) stating that the operator seeks the person's agreement to those terms." [23]

Pursuant to Paragraph 90 of the Code, OFCOM must prescribe *"the form of a notice to be given under each provision of this code that requires a notice to be given."* [24] The template notices prescribed by OFCOM,

---

[22] Ibid, Paragraph 91(6).

[23] Communications Act 2003, Schedule 3A, Paragraph 20(1) and (2).

[24] Ibid, Paragraph 90(1).

including its template Paragraph 20 notice, can be found hosted on its website.[25]

But Paragraph 20 of the Code alone, which provides for the service of a Paragraph 20 notice as a prerequisite to the acquisition of permanent code rights (after agreement has been reached with the relevant person, or a determination has been made by the Court), does not set out all the circumstances in which code operators may wish to serve a Paragraph 20 Notice.

Indeed, Paragraph 26(3) of the Code provides that *"if (and only if) the operator has given the* [relevant person] *a notice which complies with paragraph 20(2) stating that an agreement is sought on an interim basis..."* it is possible for the code operator to seek that the court grant the code operator code rights on an interim basis pending final determination (or agreement) of the terms of the code agreement.[26]

Further, Paragraph 27 of the Code provides that a Paragraph 20 notice can seek that the relevant person agree to confer code rights to a code operator on a temporary basis.[27] But this provision only applies in circumstances where telecoms apparatus is already installed on the land in question.

Importantly, it appears that the court has no power to impose code rights in a code agreement that are not expressly sought in a valid Paragraph 20 notice. This was explained by Martin Roger QC at [88] of his judgment

---

[25] See https://www.ofcom.org.uk/phones-telecoms-and-internet/information-for-industry/policy/electronic-comm-code/notices. Before prescribing these notices, OFCOM was obliged to consult wit code operators *"and such other persons as OFCOM think appropriate"* pursuant to Paragraph 90(3) of the Code.

[26] Communications Act 2003, Schedule 3A, Paragraph 26(3). In *EE Ltd v MacDonald* [2020] 3 WLUK 511 the Lands Chamber (Scotland) held that a Paragraph 20 notice seeking interim code rights does not have to specify the length of the term of the code agreement sought, as this requirement does not apply to notices, only under Paragraph 11 of the Code to code agreements (for which, see Chapter 5). This decision, albeit not binding in England and Wales, would be of general application to Paragraph 20 notices seeking code rights, interim code rights and temporary code rights.

[27] Ibid, Paragraph 27(1).

in *Cornerstone Telecommunications Infrastructure Ltd v Compton Beauchamp Estates Ltd*:

"Paragraph 20 of the Code lays down a procedure for the imposition of Code rights which the Tribunal is not free to depart from. That procedure requires the operator to identify in its notice under paragraph 20(2) inviting agreement [to] *both the Code right and "all of the other terms of the agreement that the operator seeks"... it is those rights, and no more, which the operator may apply to the Tribunal to have imposed on the unwilling occupier of the land (we say nothing at this stage about whether an application can be made for lesser rights)."*[28]

The note in parentheses should not be ignored: there is, as of yet, no authority on whether, after having served a Paragraph 20 notice, the code operator can ask the court to impose lesser rights (or rights on different terms) to what was proposed in the notice. However, we anticipate that the court will be reluctant to make such an order. The court will more likely adopt the approach taken in *EE Ltd and Hutchison 3G UK Ltd v Stephenson and AP Wireless (II) UK Ltd*,[29] where it was held that a code operator seeking to vary a code agreement is not entitled to apply for variation on terms different to what were contained in its variation notice given under Paragraph 33 of the Code.[30]

How applications for code rights, interim code rights and temporary code rights progress after the service of a valid Paragraph 20 notice is covered in Chapter 4.

The Relevant Person Under Paragraph 20

There are two classes of relevant person under Paragraph 20 of the Code, as identified by the two kinds of applications that can be made under Paragraph 20(1):

---

[28] [2019] UKUT 107 (LC). This was the first instance decision in *Compton Beauchamp*. This element of the Deputy President's judgment was not appealed, and so was not subsequently reconsidered by the Court of Appeal.

[29] [2021] UKUT 167 (LC).

[30] For which, see Chapter 9.

(1) Those who can be compelled to confer a code right on the code operator, pursuant to Paragraph 20(1)(a); and

(2) Those who can be compelled to be bound by a code right already conferred on a code operator by another, pursuant to Paragraph 20(1)(b).

The Relevant Person under Paragraph 20(1)(a)

The identity of this person is the core issue in dispute in the ongoing litigation in the case of *Cornerstone Telecommunications Infrastructure Ltd v Compton Beauchamp Estates Ltd*.[31] The facts of that case are, in summary:

(1) The landowner, Compton Beauchamp Estates Ltd ("**Compton**"), granted Vodafone a lease of land with rights of access in 2004, upon which Vodafone built a telecoms mast;

(2) The lease expired in 2014, and Vodafone thereafter continued to occupy the site under a tenancy (the species of which was also in dispute between Compton and Vodafone);

(3) From August 2014, Vodafone had been sharing use of the telecoms mast with Telefonica;

(4) Cornerstone Telecommunications Infrastructure Ltd ("**Cornerstone**") was created as a joint venture by Vodafone and Telefonica, to own and manage a portfolio of telecoms sites contributed to by both. Cornerstone subsequently became a code operator under the Code;

(5) In October 2017, Compton gave Vodafone notice to determine a tenancy at will, and sought possession of the land. Vodafone defended on the basis that it had a periodic tenancy;

[31] [2019] EWCA Civ 1755. Permission to appeal to the Supreme Court was given on 30 June 2020.

(6) Cornerstone gave Compton a Paragraph 20 notice in December 2017 (practically as soon as the Code came into force), whilst Vodafone remained in occupation of the site; and

(7) Compton refused to grant Cornerstone any code rights, or to enter into any code agreement with it, on the basis that Vodafone and not Compton was the relevant person under Paragraph 20.

Lewison LJ, who gave the leading (and unanimous) judgment of the Court of Appeal, agreed with Compton. The reason for this is that Paragraph 9 of the Code provides:

"A code right in respect of land may only be conferred on an operator by an agreement between the occupier of the land and the operator."

And because Paragraph 105 of the Code goes on to explain how:

"(1) References in this code to an occupier of land are to the occupier of land for the time being...

(5) Sub-paragraph (6) applies in relation to land which—

(a) is unoccupied, and

(b) is not a street in England and Wales or Northern Ireland or a road in Scotland.

(6) References in this code to an occupier of land, in relation to land within sub-paragraph (5), are to—

(a) the person (if any) who for the time being exercises powers of management or control over the land, or

(b) if there is no person within paragraph (a), to every person whose interest in the land would be prejudicially affected by the exercise of a code right in relation to the land."

The Court of Appeal considered it patent that, where a code operator seeks that a code right be conferred on it under Paragraph 20(1)(a), the relevant person to be given a notice under Paragraph 20(2) is *"the occupier of the land for the time being*". Under the scheme of the Code, no other person is capable of conferring a code right on a code operator (other persons are only capable of being bound by a code right already conferred by such a person).[32]

Lewison LJ then went on to clarify that, especially in the context of Paragraph 105(5) and (6) (which were not directly applicable on the facts), whether a person is an occupier of land for the purposes of the Code is *"a question of fact rather than legal status; it means physical presence on and control of the land."*[33] And, on the facts of the case, Vodafone had the relevant physical presence on and control of the land. It followed that Cornerstone's Paragraph 20 notice was invalid, as it was served on Compton instead of Vodafone.[34]

So, at present, the relevant person under Paragraph 20(1)(a) of the Code is the occupier of the land for the time being. But the final word on this issue will be had by the Supreme Court in the not-too-distant future.

<u>The Relevant Person under Paragraph 20(1)(b)</u>

The relevant person under Paragraph 20(1)(b) of the Code can be identified by reading Paragraph 20(1) – *"This paragraph applies where the operator requires a person (a "relevant person") to agree– …*

(b) to be otherwise bound by a code right which is exercisable by the operator." –

together with Paragraph 10(4) of the Code:

---

[32] See [2019] EWCA Civ 1755 at [36]-[41] generally, but in particular at [40].

[33] Ibid at [54], where Lewison LJ is directly quoting the judgment of the Martin Roger QC in the Upper Tribunal (Lands Chamber) at first instance.

[34] Lewison LJ went on to suggest that the practical way forward was for Cornerstone to serve a Paragraph 20 notice on Vodafone, for them to agree terms, and for Cornerstone to subsequently serve a Paragraph 20 notice on Compton seeking to bind it to the terms of the code agreement already extant between Cornerstone and Vodafone (as a relevant person under Paragraph 20(1)(b) of the New Code). See ibid at [89].

"The code right also binds any other person with an interest in the land who has agreed to be bound by it."

When these provisions are read together, it becomes clear that the relevant person under Paragraph 20(1)(b) of the Code is *"any other person with an interest in the land"*, where the said land is already subject to *"a code right which is exercisable by the operator"*.

Summary

In summary:

(1) Notices given by code operators must be in a prescribed form (unless relied upon by the recipient in any event), and sufficiently explain themselves in order to be valid. Notices given by other persons must be in a prescribed form (unless relied upon by the recipient in any event), with the exception of notices given in response to notices from code operators – those notices are valid even if the prescribed form is not used, but the other person sending the notice may be liable for the code operator's costs incurred as a result of failure to comply if the code operator made the other person aware of the prescribed form of notice;

(2) There is a detailed scheme for service of notices under the Code. Delivery by hand to the relevant person, by hand to their proper address, or by post (recorded or special delivery only) are valid, and service by electronic means can become valid with appropriate consent. Where the identity of the relevant person cannot be found, the notice can be served to any person on the land over which the telecoms operator wishes to acquire code rights, or by affixing it to the said land;

(3) Telecoms operators begin the process of entering code agreements by serving a Paragraph 20 notice on the relevant person. The notice needs to be in the form prescribed by OFCOM, and telecoms operators cannot seek rights in excess of what is contained in their Paragraph 20 notice;

(4) At present, it appears that the relevant person under Paragraph 21(1)(a) of the Code is the occupier of the land for the time being, which is a question of fact not of legal status. Whether this will remain the case is to be determined by the Supreme Court in the near future; and

(5) The relevant person under Paragraph 21(1)(b) of the Code is any other person with an interest in land, where that land is already subject to a code right exercisable by the code operator.

CHAPTER FOUR

THE IDENTITY OF "THE COURT", AND APPLICATIONS TO IT TO ACQUIRE CODE RIGHTS

This chapter outlines:

(1) The identity of *"the court"*;

(2) The applications that can be made by code operators to *"the court"* for it to impose code rights, interim code rights and temporary code rights on relevant persons in the absence of agreement following service of a valid Paragraph 20 notice;

(3) What test should be applied by *"the court"* when determining whether to impose code rights; and

(4) The redevelopment defence available to relevant persons who want to avoid having a code right imposed on them.

The Upper Tribunal is *"the court"*

Although the Code uses the term *"the court"* throughout,[1] the meaning of *"the court"* is prescribed by Regulation 3 of the Electronic Communications Code (Jurisdiction) Regulations 2017 (SI 2017/1284) [2] (**"the 2017 Regulations"**) as follows:

"(a) in relation to England, the First-tier Tribunal (in a case where relevant proceedings are transferred to it by the Upper Tribunal,

(b) in relation to England and Wales, the Upper Tribunal…"

---

[1] Which pursuant to Paragraphs 94(1) and (2) of Schedule 3A to the Communications Act 2003 refers to *"in relation to England and Wales the county court"* subject to any regulations made under Paragraph 95.

[2] Pursuant to Paragraph 95 of the Code.

The Upper Tribunal ("**the Tribunal**") has the power to transfer cases to the First-tier Tribunal where appropriate under Rule 5(k) of the Tribunal Procedure (Upper Tribunal) (Lands Chamber) Rules 2010 as amended [3] ("**the Rules**").

On 26 January 2018, The Honourable Mr Justice Holgate issued the Practice Note: Electronic Communications Code ("**the Practice Note**") (not a formal Practice Direction). At Paragraph 10 of the Practice Note, His Lordship noted that "*...For the time being it is not anticipated that Code disputes would normally be transferred by the Tribunal to the First-tier Tribunal, but parties who agree that their dispute should be determined in the First-tier Tribunal may apply for transfer to be considered.*"

The Practice Note recorded that proceedings which may be issued only in the Tribunal are proceedings under the following provisions of the Code:

"Part 4 (Power of the court to impose agreement)

Part 5 (Termination and modification of agreements)

Part 6 (Removal of Electronic Communications Apparatus)

Para. 53 (Alternation of apparatus at request of transport undertakers)

Part 12 (Rights to object to certain apparatus)

Part 13 (Right to lop trees)." [4]

Whereas the Tribunal does have the power to transfer relevant proceedings to the county court, should it consider the county court to be the more appropriate forum for the determination of those proceedings,[5] in practice *"the court"* will almost always be the Tribunal. At the time of writing, we are not aware of any case in which the Tribunal

[3] And now in a consolidated form, which has been in effect since 21 July 2020.

[4] The Practice Note accords entirely with Regulation 2 and 4(a) of the 2017 Regulations, the latter of which provides that proceedings under all of these parts of the Code *"must be commenced– (a) in relation to England and Wales, in the Upper Tribunal"*.

[5] Regulation 5 of the 2017 Regulations.

have opted to transfer any part of a relevant application to the county court.[6]

Applications Under Paragraph 20 of the Code: Code Rights

The requirements for a valid Paragraph 20 notice are set out in Chapter 3.

Following the service of a valid Paragraph 20 notice, pursuant to Paragraphs 20(3) and (4) of the Code, a code operator:

"(3) ... may apply to the court for an order under this paragraph if–

(a) the relevant person does not, before the end of 28 days beginning with the day on which the notice is given, agree to confer or be otherwise bound by the code right, or

(b) at any time after the notice is given, the relevant person gives notice in writing to the operator that the person does not agree to confer or otherwise be bound by the code right.

(4) An order under this paragraph is one which imposes on the operator and the relevant person an agreement between them which–

(a) confers the code right on the operator, or

(b) provides for the code right to bind the relevant person."[7]

So, if the code operator and the relevant person (identified in Chapter 3) are able to agree terms within the twenty-eight-day period after the service of the Paragraph 20 notice, no application under Paragraph 20 of the Code need be made. If this is not possible, then the code operator only acquires the ability to apply to the Tribunal after the twenty-eight-day period has expired, or after receiving notice in writing from the relevant person confirming that no agreement will be reached.

---

[6] And the Practice Note does not shed any light on when the Upper Tribunal may consider doing so.

[7] Communications Act 2003, Schedule 3A, Paragraphs 20(3) and (4).

Code agreements imposed by order under Paragraph 20 of the Code take effect as an agreement under Part 2.[8]

Applications Under Paragraph 26 of the Code: Interim Code Rights

Similarly, Paragraphs 26 of the Code provides that a code operator may apply to the Tribunal for an order imposing the conferral of interim code rights.[9] Under Paragraph 26(2), an order can provide for the code operator and relevant person to be bound by the agreement:

"(a) for the period specified in the order, or

(b) until the occurrence of an event specified in the order."[10]

Just as with an application under Paragraph 20, the Tribunal an only make an order under Paragraph 26 if the code operator has given the relevant person a Paragraph 20 notice stating that a code agreement is sought on an interim basis.[11] Further, Paragraphs 22 to 25 and 84 of the Code (which provide for the effect of a code agreement, the terms that can be imposed on parties by the Tribunal, and the payment of consideration and compensation) all apply in applications under Paragraph 26 just as they do to applications under Paragraph 20.[12]

Unlike applications under Paragraph 20, the code operator can apply to the Tribunal immediately after giving the Paragraph 20 notice, and may make an order conferring interim code rights *"if the court thinks the order should be made as a matter of urgency."*[13] Also, from the time that the period specified in the order expires, or the event specified in the order takes place, the relevant person:

[8] Ibid, Paragraph 22.

[9] Ibid, Paragraph 26(1).

[10] Ibid, Paragraph 26(2).

[11] Ibid, Paragraph 26(3).

[12] Ibid, Paragraph 26(4).

[13] Ibid, Paragraph 26(5).

"has the right, subject to and in accordance with Part 6 of this code, to require the operator to remove any electronic communications apparatus placed on the land under the agreement imposed under this paragraph." [14]

So whilst interim code rights can be applied for under similar circumstances to 'standard' Paragraph 20 applications, they can be applied for earlier, and terminate without the need for further action at the time provided for by the Tribunal.[15]

Further, the Court of Appeal have ruled that there is no requirement for an application under Paragraph 26 to be accompanied by an application under Paragraph 20: an application for interim code rights can stand on its own, if a code operator does not have need of a 'full' agreement entered into under Paragraph 20.[16]

Applications Under Paragraph 27 of the Code: Temporary Code Rights

Paragraph 27 of the Code permits a code operator to apply to the Tribunal for an order imposing *"such temporary code rights as appear reasonably necessary for securing the objective..."* [17] that:

"until the proceedings under paragraph 20 and any proceedings under paragraph 40 are determined, the service provided by the operator's network is maintained and the apparatus is properly adjusted and kept in repair." [18]

The purpose of this objective, and of Paragraph 27 as a whole, is to protect the code operator's telecoms apparatus and network in-between the termination of a relevant code agreement, and the decision of the Tribunal as to whether it will either impose a Code agreement or permit the relevant person to enforce the removal of the relevant telecoms

---

[14] Ibid, Paragraph 26(8).

[15] Ibid, Paragraph 30(3). Code agreements conferring interim code rights do not continue automatically under Paragraph 30(2) of the Code. Paragraph 30 of the Code is considered in more detail in Chapter 8.

[16] See *Cornerstone Telecommunications Infrastructure Ltd v University of London* [2019] EWCA Civ 2075.

[17] Communications Act 2003, Schedule 3A, Paragraph 27(2).

[18] Ibid, Paragraph 27(3).

apparatus from their land. The right to remove telecoms apparatus is explored in Chapter 13.

An order under Paragraph 27 can only be applied for where:

(1) A code operator has given a Paragraph 20 notice to the relevant person,[19] which requires the relevant person's agreement on a temporary basis in respect of a right which is to be exercisable in relation to telecoms equipment already installed on, under or over the land in question;[20] and

(2) The relevant person has the right to require the removal of the telecoms apparatus under Paragraph 37 or 40(1) but the code operator is not for the time being required to remove the telecoms apparatus.[21]

And just as with applications under Paragraph 26:

(1) Paragraphs 22 to 25 and 84 of the Code all apply in applications under Paragraph 27;[22] and

(2) Orders can be made on applications made before the expiry of the twenty-eight-day period for Paragraph 20 notices *"if the court thinks that the order should be made as a matter of urgency."*[23]

Just as with code agreements conferring interim code rights, code agreements conferring temporary code rights will terminate without the need for further action following the decision of the Tribunal in the proceedings brought under either Paragraph 20 or 40 of the Code.[24]

---

[19] Ibid, Paragraph 27(1)(a).

[20] Ibid, Paragraph 27(1)(b).

[21] Ibid, Paragraph 27(1)(c).

[22] Ibid, Paragraph 27(4).

[23] Ibid, Paragraph 27(5).

[24] Ibid, Paragraph 30(3). Code agreements conferring temporary code rights do not continue automatically under Paragraph 30(2) of the Code. Paragraph 30 of the Code is considered in more detail in Chapter 8.

Unlike in Paragraph 26, no specific provision is made in Paragraph 27 of the Code for temporary code rights to terminate on a certain date or event without the need for further action to be taken by either party. It would appear then that code agreements conferring temporary code rights must be terminated in the same manner as 'standard' code agreements imposed under Paragraph 20 of the Code.

The Applicable Test

The test to be applied by the Tribunal in an application under Paragraph 20 of the Code is set out in Paragraph 21:

"(1) Subject to sub-paragraph 5, the court may make an order under paragraph 20 if (and only if) the court thinks that both of the following conditions are met.

(2) The first condition is that the prejudice caused to the relevant person by the order is capable of being adequately compensated by money.

(3) The second condition is that the public benefit likely to result from the making of the order outweighs the prejudice to the relevant person.

(4) In deciding whether the second condition is met, the court must have regard to the public interest in access to a choice of high quality electronic communications services."[25]

These same conditions apply in respect of applications under Paragraph 26 of the Code, save that the Tribunal need only be satisfied that there is a *"good arguable case"* that they are made out.[26] The conditions are not relevant to applications under Paragraph 27, which fall to be determined in accordance with whether its unique objective would be secured by the grant.

Whereas the first condition requires the Tribunal to tread familiar legal ground (because there is ample guidance on whether interruption of use of land is capable of being adequately compensated in money in case law on the grant of injunctive relief), the second condition is likely to require expert evidence. In *EE Ltd and Hutchinson 3G UK Ltd v London*

[25] Ibid, Paragraph 21(1) to (4).

[26] Ibid, Paragraph 26(3)(b).

Underground Ltd,[27] which concerned an application for interim code rights over a building forming part of London Underground's operational estate, the telecoms operators produced evidence from a chartered surveyor in respect of the *"difficulties which will be created for the coverage and capacity achievable by the claimants' mobile phone networks..."* should they not be granted the interim rights.[28]

And in determining the telecoms operators' interim rights application in London Underground, Martin Roger QC made sure to highlight that *"the standard of proof will be different in any paragraph 20 application. Much more extensive rights would also be in issue and the concerns which* [the expert] *identifies in his evidence are likely to become even more acute."*[29]

The Redevelopment Defence

However, even if the above two conditions are satisfied, Paragraph 21(5) provides that:

"The court may not make an order under paragraph 20 if it thinks that the relevant person intends to redevelop all or part of the land to which the code right would relate, or any neighbouring land, and could not reasonably do so if the order were made."

This defence substantially mirrors Ground (f) of Section 30(1) of the Landlord and Tenant Act 1954 ("**the 1954 Act**"). And, to that extent, case law concerning that ground is likely to be of real assistance to relevant persons considering running the defence. The relevant person will need to establish in evidence both the settled intention to redevelop [30] and also that the redevelopment could not be reasonably carried out if the land in question were subject to the rights sought.[31]

---

27 [2021] UKUT 142 (LC).

28 Ibid, [10].

29 Ibid, [12]. Also made clear by the Court of Appeal in *Cornerstone Telecommunications Infrastructure Ltd v University of London* [2019] EWCA Civ 2075 at [77].

30 See e.g. *S Franses Ltd v Cavendish Hotel (London) Ltd [2018] UKSC 62* in respect of the requisite intention.

31 See e.g. *Leathwods Ltd v Total Oil Great Britain Ltd* [1985] 51 P&CR 20 where the proposed works of reconstruction would make it impossible, both during the

It should be noted that this defence forms part of Paragraph 21 of the Code, and so is not applicable to applications under Paragraph 27, which rise and fall on their own unique objective.

Summary

In summary:

(1) By virtue of the 2017 Regulations, *"the court"* under the Code will almost always be the Tribunal (i.e. the Upper Tribunal (Lands Chamber));

(2) Twenty-eight days after service of the Paragraph 20 notice, the code operator can apply to the Tribunal for it to impose code rights on the relevant person, if no agreement has been reached. The code operator can apply earlier if the relevant person writes to them making clear no agreement will be reached before the twenty-eight-day period expires;

(3) Code operators can apply to the Tribunal for it to impose interim code rights on the relevant person any time after service of a Paragraph 20 notice seeking interim code rights. An application made before the twenty-eight-day period expires will be entertained if sufficiently urgent. Interim code rights terminate without further action on the date, or after the event, prescribed by the Tribunal;

(4) Where there is already telecoms apparatus on the land, and the relevant person has the right to require it be removed, a code operator can serve a Paragraph 20 notice and then apply to the Tribunal for temporary code rights pending the determination of any application under Paragraph 20. An application made before the twenty-eight-day period expires will be entertained if sufficiently urgent;

(5) The Tribunal will impose code rights provided the telecoms operator can satisfy two conditions: (1) that any prejudice to the relevant person is capable of being adequately compensated in money, and (2)

---

redevelopment and after it was complete, for the tenant to carry on his business from the premises.

that the public benefit likely to arise from the making of the order outweighs the prejudice to the relevant person;

(6) Interim code rights will be imposed provided that the telecoms operator can show a good arguable case that those two conditions are made out;

(7) Neither code rights nor interim code rights will be granted if the relevant person can establish the defence that they intend to redevelop all or part of the land to which the code right(s) would relate, or any neighbouring land, and could not reasonably do so if the order were made; and

(8) Whether temporary code rights are to be granted is subject to its own unique objective, namely whether the grant is reasonably necessary to secure the continued maintenance of the code operator's telecoms network, or the repair and adjustment of their apparatus, pending the outcome of their Paragraph 20 application.

CHAPTER FIVE

TERMS OF AND FORMALITIES FOR CODE AGREEMENTS, AND ENFORCEMENT

In this chapter, we explain:

(1) The terms that must be included in a code agreement imposed by the Tribunal;

(2) The Tribunal's discretion to include other terms in an imposed code agreement;

(3) The formalities required for a code agreement that has either been agreed or had its terms determined by the Tribunal; and

(4) How code agreements and code rights are enforced.

Mandatory Terms for Imposed Code Agreements

Whereas the Code does not limit the scope of the terms that can be included in code agreements entered voluntarily (save for the formalities considered below), Paragraph 23 of the Code outlines the scope of the terms that the Tribunal can impose:

"(1) An order under paragraph 20 may impose an agreement which gives effect to the code right sought by the operator with such modifications as the court thinks appropriate.

(2) An order under paragraph 20 must require the agreement to contain such terms as the court thinks appropriate, subject to sub-paragraphs (3) to (8).

(3) The terms of the agreement must include terms as to the payment of consideration by the operator to the relevant person for the relevant person's agreement to confer or be bound by the code right (as the case may be).

(4) Paragraph 24 makes provision about the determination of consideration under sub-paragraph (3).

(5) The terms of the agreement must include the terms the court thinks appropriate for ensuring that the least possible loss and damage is caused by the exercise of the code right to persons who–

(a) occupy the land in question,

(b) own interests in that land, or

(c) are from time to time on that land.

(6) Sub-paragraph (5) applies in relation to a person regardless of whether the person is a party to the agreement.

(7) The terms of the agreement must include terms specifying how long the code right conferred by the agreement is exercisable.

(8) The court must determine whether the terms of the agreement should include a term–

(a) permitting termination of the agreement (and, if so, in what circumstances);

(b) enabling the relevant person to require the operator to reposition or temporarily remove the electronic communications equipment to which the agreement relates (and, if so, in what circumstances)."

So, when considering what terms to impose on the parties, the Tribunal must both have regard to ensuring that the *"least possible loss and damage"* is caused by the grant,[1] and also (regardless of whether such terms are proffered in the Paragraph 20 notice) whether to impose terms relating to termination of the agreement and repositioning or removal of the telecoms apparatus.[2] In any event, the Tribunal must impose the

[1] Communications Act 2003, Schedule 3A, Paragraph 23(5)..

[2] Ibid, Paragraph 23(8).

payment of consideration [3] and specify the period for which the code right will be exercisable.[4]

Further, the Tribunal has the power to modify the code right sought in the Paragraph 20 notice, granting the code operator something different to what it sought,[5] and it must require the code agreement to contain any other terms that it thinks appropriate.[6]

Finally, it should be noted that all of the above also applies to any applications made under Paragraphs 26 and 27 of the Code in respect of interim or temporary code rights.[7]

Discretionary Terms for Imposed Code Agreements

The extent of the discretion to impose other terms on the code operator and relevant person under Paragraph 23(2) of the Code was considered by the Tribunal in *Cornerstone Telecommunications Infrastructure Ltd v Keast*.[8]

In Cornerstone's Paragraph 20 notice it sought a number of terms be included in the proposed code agreement that were not code rights, including:

(1) Warranties and a covenant for quiet enjoyment to be entered by Mr Keast;

(2) The right for Cornerstone to install a generator on the relevant land;

(3) The right for Cornerstone to compel Mr Keast to enter into agreements with third parties, and to restrict his ability to negotiate with them;

[3] Ibid, Paragraph 23(3) and (4).

[4] Ibid, Paragraph 23(7).

[5] Ibid, Paragraph 23(1).

[6] Ibid, Paragraph 23(2).

[7] Ibid, Paragraphs 26(4)(c) and 27(4)(c).

[8] [2019] UKUT 116 (LC).

(4) A right for Cornerstone to restrict Mr Keast's access to the relevant land;

(5) Covenants on the part of Mr Keast to maintain the condition of his farm and protect the land from interference;

(6) Covenants on the part of Mr Keast to notify Cornerstone of various matters;

(7) Covenants on the part of Mr Keast not to interfere with the relevant land or authorise any interference with it; and

(8) A restriction on Mr Keast's ability to develop other parts of his property.

The Tribunal considered the meaning and effect of Paragraph 23(2) of the Code, and concluded that:

"... paragraph 23 contains no restriction upon the terms that may be imposed, although sub-paragraphs (3) to (8) set out what they must include.

Clearly in deciding what it thinks appropriate the Tribunal will have very careful regard to the overall scheme of the Code, which provides for the imposition of Code rights and other terms on occupiers of land at a rate of consideration far lower than was payable under the old code. The Tribunal will have in mind the need to be fair to both parties, and what is "appropriate" is likely to be influenced by the basis of consideration that it can impose. It may be considered inappropriate to impose on a site provider certain obligations intended to facilitate the provision of the operator's network when the consideration receivable by the site provider is to be unrelated to the value of that network.

But there is no principled reason why there should not be, for example, a restriction on the landowner's right of access to the site, in the interests of safety, or a restriction on the landowner's ability to give others access to the site. Whether there is any scope for the imposition of positive obligations on the landowner is a difficult question and one might expect that it would be a rare occurrence. But it is not outside the Tribunal's jurisdiction. I see no reason to regard any terms to which the Respondent points as outside the

Tribunal's jurisdiction, although there are some that it might well, in the exercise of its discretion, refuse to impose." [9]

As the *Keast* litigation concerned preliminary issues, rather than a final determination of the terms to be imposed, the Tribunal did not go on to specify which of the terms proposed by Cornerstone in its Paragraph 20 notice it would grant or refuse. However, the Tribunal's position on the scope of its discretion is clear: the discretion is wide, and how it is exercised is most likely to be informed by the nature of the consideration it can and will award under Paragraph 24 of the Code.[10]

The exercise of the discretion found in Paragraph 23(2) of the Code was also considered by the Tribunal in *Cornerstone Telecommunications Infrastructure Ltd v London and Quadrant Housing Trust*. [11] In that case, Cornerstone wanted to acquire code rights to install equipment on the roof of an eighty-storey block containing both offices and residential flats. The roof already housed solar panels, and the apparatus would be installed around them.

The housing trust was concerned about the effect of increased weight on the roof, and argued that the Tribunal should impose a term in the code agreement prescribing an 'equipment cap' limiting Cornerstone's code rights to protect the integrity of the building.[12] Further, Cornerstone argued that the wording of Paragraph 23(2) suggests (because the Tribunal should impose *"an agreement which gives effect to the code right sought by the operator…"*) that the starting point for the Tribunal should be the terms proposed by the code operator, and that the relevant person must justify any departure therefrom.

Dealing with these arguments in reverse, the Tribunal concluded that:

---

[9] Ibid, [56]-[58].

[10] For which, see Chapter 6.

[11] [2020] UKUT 282 (LC).

[12] The issue of equipment caps have been something of a flashpoint for the exercise of the discretion at Paragraph 23(2) of the New Code, given that one was also argued for by the relevant person in *Cornerstone Telecommunications Infrastructure Ltd v University of the Arts London* [2020] UKUT 248 (LC): see e.g. [130].

(1) The starting point for formulating the agreement to be imposed is the code right itself, which should not be modified unless the Tribunal considers it appropriate to do so under Paragraph 23(1). As for the other terms of the code agreement, these are subject to a wide discretion with no presumption in favour of the code operator's proposed terms;[13] and

(2) That the housing trust's fear that Cornerstone might install unlimited equipment on the roof of the building, threatening its integrity, was *"fanciful"* given that the agreed terms included a term prohibiting Cornerstone *"from overloading any part of the building, and requiring it to take all reasonable steps to ensure that it does not make the building or any plant or machinery on it unsafe"*.

The Tribunal also clarified that Paragraph 23(5) of the Code is not a *"prohibition on the imposition of code rights which may cause loss and damage to the owners and occupiers of land. It is a direction to the Tribunal to incorporate terms intended to minimise loss and damage as part of an agreement which will also include terms as to consideration assessed under para.24 and rights to compensation for loss and damage for the site provider and others under paras 25, 44 and 84."*[14] This approach to Paragraph 23(5) substantially mirrors the approach towards Paragraph 23(2) adopted in *Keast*.

Formalities for All Code Agreements

Regardless of whether a code agreement has been entered into freely by the code operator and the relevant person, or has had its terms imposed on them by the Tribunal, it must comply with all of the formalities set out in Paragraph 11 of the Code:

"(1) An agreement under this Part–

(a) must be in writing,

(b) must be signed by or on behalf of the parties to it,

[13] [2020] UKUT 282 (LC) at [43].

[14] Ibid, [48].

(c) must state for how long the code right is exercisable, and

(d) must state the period of notice (if any) required to terminate the agreement."[15]

The Part of the Code this refers to is Part 2. Any code agreement entered into pursuant to the Code is considered to be an agreement under Part 2 of the Code.[16]

These formalities also apply to code agreements that have been varied, whether consensually or under Paragraph 34 of the Code:[17]

"(2) Sub-paragraph (1)(a) and (b) also applies to the variation of an agreement under this Part.

(3) The agreement as varied must still comply with sub-paragraph (1)(c) and (d)."[18]

The Code does not contain any express provision setting out the consequences of failing to comply with these formalities. Presumably, failure to comply with the formalities would render the agreement not *"An agreement under this Part"* i.e., not a code agreement. A potential consequence of this is considered below.

Enforcement of Code Rights and Agreements

Pursuant to Paragraph 93 of the Code:

"An agreement under this code, and any right conferred by this code, may be enforced–

(a) in the case of an agreement imposed by a court or tribunal, by the court or tribunal which imposed the agreement,

(b) in the case of any agreement or right, by any court or tribunal which for the time being has the power to impose an agreement under this code, or

[15] Communications Act 2003, Schedule 3A, Paragraph 11(1).

[16] This becomes relevant in the context of Part 5 of the Code (see Chapter 8) and the transitional provisions between the Old Code and the Code (see Chapter 12).

[17] Variation of code agreements is considered in Chapter 12.

[18] Commination's Act 2003, Schedule 3A, Paragraph 11(2)-(3).

(c) in the case of any agreement or right, by any court of competent jurisdiction."

It should be noted that Paragraph 93 of the Code is not drafted and/or. It therefore follows that:

(1) An imposed code agreement should be enforced in the court or tribunal that imposed it; else

(2) A code agreement entered voluntarily (or a code agreement imposed by a court or tribunal which is no longer extant) should be enforced in the court or tribunal with the power to impose code agreements; else

(3) Where there is no longer a court or tribunal with the power to impose code agreements, they should be enforced in any court of competent jurisdiction.[19]

In practice, by virtue of the 2017 Regulations,[20] code agreements and code rights whether entered voluntarily or imposed are likely to be enforceable in the Tribunal.

One situation where this would not be the case would be where a code agreement has been imposed in (for example) the county court, because the Tribunal opted to transfer an application under Paragraph 20 there pursuant to its power under Regulation 5 of the 2017 Regulations.

Another is where a code operator and relevant person have entered into an agreement that purports to be a code agreement but does not comply with all of the formalities contained in Paragraph 11 of the Code. If that agreement is not properly considered a code agreement as a consequence of that failure, it would not be enforceable under Paragraph 93 of the

---

[19] This analysis, although not yet tested in the Upper Tribunal or the courts, marries with Regulation 4 of the Electronic Communications Code (Jurisdiction) Regulations 2017, which (by virtue of Paragraph 93 being contained in Part 16 of the Code) does not mandate that enforcement applications under Paragraph 93 of the Code be brought in the Tribunal. So there must be some circumstances under which enforcement applications under the Code can be issued in an another forum.

[20] Electronic Communications Code (Jurisdiction) Regulations 2017 (SI 2017/1284). See Chapter 4.

Code. Instead, it would have to be enforced in any court with the requisite jurisdiction to determine contractual disputes generally.

Summary

In summary:

(1) The mandatory terms for imposed code agreements include payment of consideration and the period of the agreement. The Tribunal must also have regard to causing the least possible loss to the relevant person and other third parties (subject to the ability to order consideration and compensation be paid), and whether to include terms providing for early termination and the repositioning or removal of apparatus by either party;

(2) The Tribunal has a wide discretion to order that the code agreement contain other terms that it considers appropriate;

(3) All code agreements must comply with four core formalities. They must be in writing, be signed by or on behalf of the parties, state the period of the agreement, and state the period of notice require to terminate the agreement (if any); and

(4) In almost all cases, disputes related to the enforcement of extant code agreements under the Code fall under the jurisdiction of the Tribunal.

CHAPTER SIX

CONSIDERATION AND VALUATION

This Chapter considers four topics:

(1) The policy underpinning consideration under the Code

(2) The circumstances in which there is an obligation to pay consideration under the Code;

(3) The method of valuation of the consideration under the Code; and

(4) The valuation of rent for telecoms equipment under Section 34 of the 1954 Act.[1]

It should be noted that compensation is not addressed in this chapter, but in Chapter 7.

The Policy Underpinning Consideration Under the Code

In order to understand the approach taken to consideration in the Code it is necessary to consider the background against which the Code was drafted and the policy underpinning the code.[2] Ed Vaizey, the Minister of State for Culture and the Digital Economy confirmed in the forward to his ministerial statement in May 2016 '*A New Electronic Communications Code*':

"*It will make major reforms to the rights that communications providers have to access land – moving to a "no scheme" basis of valuation regime. This will ensure property owners will be fairly compensated for use of their land, but also explicitly acknowledge the economic value for all of society created from investment in digital infrastructure. In this respect, it will put digital communications infrastructure on a similar regime to utilities like electricity*

[1] Landlord and Tenant Act 1954.

[2] For which generally, see Chapter 1.

and water. This will help deliver the coverage that is needed, even in hard to reach areas."

The May 2016 ministerial statement directly addressed the method of assessing consideration. In the section entitled '*Government response: How Consideration is to be Determined*' it was recorded that the Law Commission review in 2013 led to recommendations which were directed towards tackling '*ransom rents*'. The ministerial statement continued to note that while site providers should get "*fair value for the use of their land*" that "*this should not, as a matter of principle, include a share of the economic value created by very high public demand for services that the operator provides.*" As a result, the proposal was to limit consideration in the new scheme by adopting a 'no scheme' rule in order to "*encourage greater investment and improved network coverage.*"

The Obligation to Pay Consideration

The requirement to pay consideration differs depending on whether the parties have reached an agreement or referred the matter to the court.

Part 2 of the Code makes provision regarding the conferral of code rights, those who are bound by such rights and the exercise of code rights. When agreements are reached consensually pursuant to Part 2 of the Code, the formalities in Paragraph 11 of the Code must be completed.[3] But there is no provision there requiring the payment of consideration. In practice such compensation would usually be agreed.

Where no agreement is reached between the code operator and the relevant person, Part 4 of the Code confers power on the court to impose an agreement.[4] When the matter is referred to the Tribunal, pursuant to Part 4 of the Code the obligation to pay consideration is mandatory. By Paragraph 23(3) of the Code the agreement must provide terms for the payment of consideration by the operator to the relevant person in return for that person conferring or being bound by the code right.

By Paragraph 24(4) of the Code, the terms imposed by the court may be for consideration to be payable as a lump sum or periodically. Payment

---

[3] For which, see Chapter 5.

[4] For which, see Chapter 4.

may also be on the occurrence of a specified event or events or otherwise as the Tribunal may direct.

The Valuation Method

As Part 2 of the Code is silent regarding consideration in cases in which an agreement has been reached, it follows that the parties can freely adopt whatever method of calculation they choose to calculate consideration.

In those cases where the powers of the court are invoked under Part 4 of the Code, there is no freedom to adopt the method of calculation the parties choose. Paragraph 24 of the Code specifies the formula for calculating consideration. That is the only formula which may be used and requires the valuation criteria and assumptions specified at Paragraph 24(1) to (3) of the Code to be utilised: see *EE Ltd and Hutchinson 3G Ltd v London Borough of Islington* [5] at [60].

By Paragraph 24(1) of the Code, the consideration "*must be an amount or amounts representing the market value of the relevant person's agreement to confer or be bound by the code right (as the case may be).*"

This definition of "*market value*" departs from the usual definition of 'market rent', which was usually a price agreed by a willing buyer and willing seller in an arm's length transaction. Instead, this now focuses upon the value of the agreement to only one of the parties – the seller. This was considered by Martin Rodger QC in his judgment in *London Borough of Islington* at [60]-[62] and was described there as "*a surprising formulation*".

In *London Borough of Islington* at [63], Martin Rodger QC considered whether there may have been an intention to signal an application of the principles used in compensation for compulsory purchase, namely that any value attributable solely to the scheme of the authority which proposed to acquire land compulsorily must be left out of account. This was the *Point Gourde* principle derived from the House of Lords decision in *Pointe Gourde Quarrying and Transport Co Ltd v Sub-Intendent of Crown Lands.*[6] This established that any additional value which was

[5] [2019] UKUT 0053.

[6] [1947] AC 565.

existed only because of the intention of the relevant authority was to be disregarded.

However, Paragraph 24(1) of the Code is subject to the detailed definition of "*market value*" in Paragraph 24(2) of the Code which provides that it is:

"*For this purpose the market value of a person's agreement to confer or be bound by a code right is subject to sub-paragraph (3), the amount that, at the date the market value is assessed, a willing buyer would pay a willing seller for the agreement—*

(a) in a transaction at arm's length,

(b) on the basis that the buyer and seller were acting prudently and with full knowledge of the transaction, and

(c) on the basis that the transaction was subject to the other provisions of the agreement imposed by the order under paragraph 20."

On this basis Martin Rodger QC considered it as giving "*an entirely conventional shape to the exercise*" [7] citing Lord Hoffman in *IRC v Gray (Executor of Lady Fox)*: [8]

"*It cannot be too strongly emphasised that although the sale is hypothetical, there is nothing hypothetical about the open market in which it is supposed to have taken place. The concept of the open market involves assuming that the whole world was free to bid, and then forming a view about what in those circumstances would in real life have been the best price reasonably obtainable...*"

What is critical to the assessment is the introduction of the assumptions contained in Paragraph 24(3) of the Code, which requires that the market value "*must be assessed on these assumptions*", namely:

"*(a) that the right that the transaction relates to does not relate to the provision or use of an electronic communications network;*

[7] [2019] UKUT 0053 at [64].

[8] [1994] STC 360.

(b) that paragraphs 16 and 17 (assignment, and upgrading and sharing) do not apply to the right or any apparatus to which it could apply;

(c) that the right in all other respects corresponds to the code right;

(d) that there is more than one site which the buyer could use for the purpose for which the buyer seeks the right.

In London Borough of Islington at [66], the Tribunal described the first of these assumptions as "*the most significant*" and adopted the term the "*no-network*" assumption to describe it. The no-network assumption eliminates any argument by the occupier that the compensation should be commensurate with the potential profit the code operator will make as a telecoms network provider. No value arising from the intention of the code operator to use the site as part of its network is permitted.[9] The relevant person is prevented from factoring in any ransom. This is extremely favourable to the code operator, and is a material and deliberate departure from the position prior to the Code.

The second assumption is that Paragraphs 16 and 17 of the Code do not apply.[10]

The third assumption is that the right in all other respects corresponds to the code right. In London Borough of Islington the Tribunal considered this assumption and held at [70] that:

"It has already been provided by para.24(2) that market value means the amount which would be agreed for rights conferred on the same terms as are provided for by the agreement being imposed, and it may therefore be that this assumption adds nothing of substance. It will be a question of fact in each case what use may be made of the site on the terms imposed, having regard to the no- network assumption. In this case the agreement to be imposed includes a covenant by the operator not to use the site other than for the permitted use of providing the networks of its shareholders. Despite the narrowness of the permitted use both parties approached the issue of valuation on the assumption that the rooftop site could be used for open storage. Once again, in this case we heard no evidence or detailed argument about para.24(3)(c)

[9] See [2019] UKUT 0053 at [68].

[10] For which, see Chapter 2.

and we have reached no final conclusion on its potential effect, but we agree with the parties' implicit acknowledgement that the no-network assumption must permit some notional relaxation of contractual terms which would otherwise limit the permitted use to statutory Code purposes only. In principle, therefore, we do not think it is impermissible to have regard to rental values achieved for other uses even where the only permitted use under the imposed agreement is a Code use."

The fourth and final assumption is that there is more than one site which the buyer could use. The purpose of this is to stop any monopoly of sites and prevent any impact on value to be caused by lack of suitable land.

In *London Borough of Islington*, the Tribunal reached a number of key conclusions on the approach to be taken to valuing the consideration under the Code:

(1) That there was no obligation upon the valuer to assume that the market in which the transaction occurs is competitive;[11]

(2) That the price was not necessarily nominal because there was only one bidder in the market;[12]

(3) The willing buyer cannot use the absence of demand to drive the price down to a level at which the seller would be not willing to transaction;[13]

(4) If the reality is that the nature of the premises is such that no one would pay anything for it then the market value may be nominal;[14] and

(5) That it was wrong to approach the assessment of consideration either on the basis that the absence of competition must necessarily result

---

[11] [2019] UKUT 0053 at [83].

[12] Ibid, at [84] citing *FR Evans (Leeds) Ltd v English Electric Co Ltd* (1978) 36 P&CR 185 and *Raja Vyricherla Narayana Gajapatiraju v The Revenue Divisional Officer Vizagapotam* [1939] AC 302 at 316.

[13] [2019] UKUT 0053 at [86].

[14] [2019] UKUT 0053 at [87]-[90].

> in a nominal value or that the assumption of a willing buyer would lead to a figure which was more than nominal.[15]

The Tribunal considered the value of the land in every case depended "*on its characteristics and potential uses and not simply on the number of potential bidders in the market.*"[16] The site provider in London Borough of Islington was be taken to be the landlord of all of the occupiers in the building and to owe contractual and statutory duties to them (and that such occupiers may not welcome telecommunications equipment on the roof, potentially creating an additional administrative burden for the landlord) because those were the facts on the ground in that case.[17]

It was necessary to give effect to the no-network assumption, which meant that the purpose for which the rights are granted was assumed to have nothing to do with the provision of or use of a telecoms network.[18] As a result, it was not appropriate to use transactions under the Old Code as comparables.[19] The Tribunal also held that there was no presumption of a minimum amount payable before the willing seller would sell because there was a need to assume a transaction,[20] and that there was no increased level of consideration to reflect the acquisition of a right to install up to three additional dish antennae in the future as this was contrary to the no-network assumption.[21] Although there was no demand for space on the roof of the ten-storey residential building for any commercial purpose unconnected to telecommunications, that did not dictate a nominal consideration.[22]

---

15 Ibid, at [91].

16 Ibid.

17 [2019] UKUT 0053 at [93].

18 Ibid, at [94].

19 Ibid, at [95]. There were a number of reasons for this: this approach failed to apply the no-network assumption; was based upon a different statutory valuation hypothesis; were historic values; the use of indexation over such a long period of time was unreliable; the transactions relied upon were those in which the site provider was not represented.

20 Ibid, at [96].

21 Ibid, at [97].

22 Ibid, at [98].

The Tribunal considered that the case was unlike the case of *Port of London Authority v Transport for London* [23] because a lease granting code rights was not a freehold sale which divests the seller of all interest in the site. Rather, it restricted what the respondent may do with the building (for example the apparatus needed to be resituated during works to the roof) and so the additional risks and obligations that the relationship created for the site provider must be taken into account.[24]

The Tribunal also considered that the case was not like *Hoare v National Trust* [25] or *Telereal Trillium v Hewitt* [26] in which a notional letting transferred expensive liabilities from the landlord to the tenant. While the seller was assumed to be willing, it wanted the best price payable and since the inconvenience of the equipment being situated on the roof was not offset by any benefit it was likely that the parties would agree that this should be reflected in the compensation payable.[27]

The Tribunal did agree with both parties that the code operator should make a contribution towards the costs and expenses of running the building and complying with its obligations. However, it regarded this as consideration rather than as compensation.[28]

The Tribunal also held that the consideration figure should take into account the fact that the terms sought, and which the Tribunal was to impose, did not include an annual service charge, and that the consideration payable to offset this should be less than the sum paid by individual leaseholders since some of the services they enjoyed would not be used by the code operator; a contribution towards roof repairs could also be taken into account.[29]

---

[23] [2008] RVR 93.

[24] [2019] UKUT 0053 at [99].

[25] (1999) 77 P&CR 366.

[26] [2018] EWCA Civ 26.

[27] [2019] UKUT 0053 at [100].

[28] Ibid, at [101].

[29] Ibid, at [102]-[105].

In conclusion, by an application of the relevant factors, the Tribunal assessed the appropriate consideration to be £1000 per annum.

In *Cornerstone Telecommunications Infrastructure Ltd v London and Quadrant Housing Trust* [30] the Tribunal emphasised that certain matters would necessarily be included in most cases where consideration was being assessed, namely:

(1) The current or alternative (non-network) use value which required that the value of the site as part of an operator's network was to be disregarded, but not its value to any other potential tenant;

(2) The value to the tenant of any additional benefits conferred by the letting; and

(3) The expense to the site provider of the operator using the site for the apparatus which could form additional consideration or compensation.[31]

The Tribunal noted that the additional stages of consideration set out below from *Vodafone Ltd v Hanover Capital Ltd* [32] were not necessary where an agreement was imposed by the Tribunal because compensation could be awarded for legal expenses and rent negotiations, and no addition to reflect an inducement was permissible.[33]

The three-stage test identified in *London and Quadrant* was approved in *On Tower UK Ltd v J H and F W Green Ltd*.[34] The case involved the first decision under the Code of a valuation of a rural greenfield site. The site was located on an estate which had mixed use of residential and agricultural buildings. The Claimant was holding over and the Tribunal had to consider whether equipment and sharing rights should be limited and the annual rent. The Tribunal considered that the annual rent for

30 [2020] UKUT 282 (LC).

31 Ibid, [134]-[137].

32 [2021] 2 P&CR 3.

33 [2020] UKUT 282 (LC) at [105].

34 [2020] UKUT 348 (LC). An appeal is outstanding on this case at the time of writing.

the site was £1200 to reflect the proximity of residential buildings. It would have been £750 without the proximity of the residential buildings.

The Valuation of Rent for Telecoms Equipment Under Section 34 of the 1954 Act

In *Hanover Capital*, a subsisting agreement [35] was protected under Part 2 of the 1954 Act, and so the new rent had to be determined in accordance with Section 34 of the 1954 Act rather than the Code. So, the court was required to consider the rent in the open market, there being disregarded any effect on rent of Vodafone's occupation, goodwill attributable to its business, and improvements. The key valuation assumptions were:

(1) That the site was in the condition it was in *"if the actual tenant had removed fixtures installed by it and complied with its obligations"* and *"as it was before the... lease was granted"*;[36]

(2) That the hypothetical tenant was a code operator *"because the terms of the tenancy say so and the only permitted use of the Site under those terms is for Code purposes"*;[37]

(3) That both negotiating parties were prudent and knowledgeable, including of the hypothetical tenant's rights under the Code;[38]

(4) The rent would be the only quantified sum payable;[39]

(5) The negotiation would be fair and friendly. The parties were assumed to be willing but not anxious to do a deal;[40] and

(6) It was noted that the process for negotiating terms for mast sites was fundamentally different to other property transactions, and that the real-world market was not the open market required under Section 34 of the 1954 Act.[41] The non-network assumption required by

---

[35] For which, see Chapter 12.

[36] [2021] 2 P&CR 3 at [50].

[37] Ibid, at [51].

[38] Ibid, at [51]-[52].

[39] Ibid, at [54].

[40] Ibid, at [57].

[41] Ibid, at [69]-[71].

Paragraph 24 of the Code formed the backdrop to the hypothetical negotiations.[42]

And the following six topics were considered *a "helpful framework"* in replicating the factors that would influence the parties in a case like *Hanover Capital*:

(1) The alternative use value of the site which would be the equivalent of the rental value of the site for the most valuable non-operator use;

(2) An allowance to reflect any additional benefit conferred on the tenant by the letting;

(3) An adjustment to reflect any greater adverse effect of the letting on the willing lessor than the alternative use on which the existing use value was based;

(4) The fees payable by the hypothetical landlord for negotiating the rent with the hypothetical tenant's representatives;

(5) Conveyancing legal fees; and

(6) The possibility that the hypothetical tenant would pay an additional sum to induce the landlord to enter into the letting.[43]

Summary

In summary:

(1) The policy objective of an expansion of the network coverage is critical to understanding and applying the Code;

(2) The parties are free to reach agreements under Part 2 of the Code as long as the formalities in Paragraph 11 are completed. When they do so they are free to agree the payment of consideration, and usually do so, although it is not mandatory;

(3) Where no agreement is reached the Tribunal has power to impose an agreement. In such cases there is an obligation to pay consideration.

[42] Ibid, at [87].

[43] [2021] 2 P&CR 3 at [89].

Consideration may be paid as a lump sum, periodically or on occurrence of a particular event;

(4) Under Part 2 of the Code the parties can adopt whatever method of valuation they wish to adopt. Under Part 4 of the Code the calculation specified in Paragraph 24 must be used, which includes a series of assumptions including the no-network assumption, and assumption that more than one site can be used thus preventing the site provider from obtaining a ransom; and

(5) In conducting the valuation transactions under the Old Code cannot be used as appropriate comparables.

CHAPTER SEVEN
COMPENSATION

This Chapter considers nine topics:

(1) The power to award compensation under the Code;

(2) The order for compensation;

(3) The timing of the award for compensation;

(4) The limitation on compensation;

(5) The heads of compensation;

(6) Legal and valuation expenses;

(7) Diminution in value;

(8) Other claims for compensation; and

(9) Evidence.

It should be noted that consideration is not addressed in this chapter, but in Chapter 6.

The Power to Make an Order for Compensation

The parts of the Code which deal with compensation are Paragraph 25 and Part 14, which contains Paragraphs 83 to 86 of the Code.

By Paragraph 25(1) of the Code the Tribunal may make an order requiring the operator to pay compensation to the relevant person for any loss and damage which has been sustained or will be sustained by that person as a result of the code right to which the order relates. Accordingly, the power of the Tribunal to order compensation is dependent on the order being made pursuant to Paragraph 20.

Part 14 of the Code makes additional provision regarding compensation. Paragraph 84(1) provides that Paragraph 84 of the Code applies in two circumstances:

(1) Where the power of the court is exercised pursuant to Paragraph 25(1) of the Code, imposing a code agreement on a person; and

(2) Where the power is exercised in Paragraph 44(5) of the Code for compensation in relation to the removal of apparatus from the land.[1]

Paragraph 84 of the Code does not apply where there is a consensual agreement to confer Code rights pursuant to Part 2.[2]

Part 14 of the Code also makes provision for compensation for injurious affection to neighbouring land in a case where an operator exercises a right conferred by Parts 2 to 9 of the Code.[3] The compensation is payable under Section 10 of the Compulsory Purchase Act 1965, and is payable irrespective of whether the person claiming the compensation has any interest in the land. The compensation is payable in relation to loss or damage sustained as a result of the code operator exercising code rights.

In *EE Ltd and Hutchinson 3G Ltd v London Borough of Islington* [4] the Tribunal considered that the provisions of the Code relating to consideration were "*very flexible*". However, the Tribunal rejected a submission that the power was also discretionary. The Tribunal considered that the provisions of Paragraph 25 of the Code were expressed in terms which reflected the fact that in certain cases no compensation was required because there was no loss or damage sustained as a result of the exercise of code rights.[5] But where loss or damage was sustained the Tribunal did not consider that relief could be refused.

The Order for Compensation

By Paragraph 25(3) of the Code, the order for compensation may either specify the amount of compensation to be paid to the code operator or give directions for determination of the amount.

---

[1] For which, see Chapter 10.

[2] Confirmed by the Tribunal in *EE Ltd and Hutchinson 3G Ltd v London Borough of Islington* [2019] UKUT 0053 at [144].

[3] Parts 7 to 9 falling outside the scope of this book.

[4] [2019] UKUT 0053.

[5] Ibid, at [109].

The directions may provide for the amount of the compensation to be agreed between the code operator and the relevant person, or for the dispute about quantum to be determined by arbitration.[6] Further, pursuant to Paragraph 25(5) of the Code, the code operator may be required to make the payment in a number of different ways: by a lump payment; periodic payments; a payment "*on the occurrence of an event or events*"; and there is also a broad power to order that payment be made "*in such other form or at such other time or times as the court may direct.*"

The Timing of the Award

Once the power is triggered it can be exercised either at the time an order under Paragraph 20 is made, or at any time afterwards on the application of the relevant person.[7]

In *London Borough of Islington*, the Tribunal rejected a submission that the award of compensation may only be made at the time the order imposing the code agreement was made. The Tribunal considered that this was contrary to the intention of Paragraph 25(2)(b) of the Code, which allowed the order to be made "*at any times afterwards*", and contrary to the intended flexibility of the Code.[8] Further, the Tribunal considered that this would have the unjust consequence of meaning the site provider had to shoulder the burden of any unanticipated loss.

Limitation on Compensation

Under Paragraph 86 of the Code, provided the code operator is lawfully exercising rights conferred by the Code, it is protected from liability for loss and damage caused by the lawful exercise of any right conferred by the Code, except as provided by the Code. While this apparently prohibits any claims for compensation, save under the Code, it should be noted that this is expressly in relation to "*lawful*" exercise of rights.

We anticipate that there may be arguments about compensation in cases in which it is alleged that there was an unlawful exercise of rights, and what constitutes the "*unlawful*" use of code rights in due course. We

---

[6] Communications Act 2003, Schedule 3A, Paragraph 25(4).

[7] Ibid, Paragraph 25(2).

[8] [2019] UKUT 0053 at [111].

predict that there are two potential ways in which the courts might interpret seek to Paragraph 86:

(1) Purposively, maintaining that a high threshold is required to consider that conduct of an operator was "*unlawful*" such that the limitation upon seeking compensation would not apply. This is because, as stated repeatedly by the courts in a number of cases considered in this book, the Code is intended to be a comprehensive scheme; or

(2) Strictly, such that any (for example) breach of contract is an "*unlawful*" act. This would mean that a code operator who exercises a code right in a manner prohibited under the code agreement (such as where a code right is only exercisable between certain hours of the day) and causes loss to the site provider by doing so would in principle be liable to compensate the site provider in damages for breach of contract.

Which approach will be adopted by the courts remains to be seen.

It should also be noted that there is no right to double recovery. It is clear from *London Borough of Islington* that double counting is not permissible.[9] So, matters taken into account under the heading of consideration may not be claimed a second time as compensation. This is particularly pertinent to diminution in value (for which, see below). In *London Borough of Islington* it was held that the site provider was not entitled to compensation for diminution in value of the land. Rather, that sum should be reflected in the consideration payable; only to the extent that such diminution is not so reflected can a separate claim be made for compensation.

Heads of Compensation

The heads of compensation in Paragraph 84(2) of the Code depend upon the circumstances of the case. But the power extends to:

"*(a) expenses (including reasonable legal and valuation expenses, subject to the provisions of any enactment about the powers of the court by whom the order for compensation is made to award costs…*

---

[9] Also see *Cornerstone Telecommunications Infrastructure Ltd v London & Quadrant Housing Trust* [2020] UKUT 0282 (LC) at [99].

(b) diminution in value of the land, and

(c) costs of reinstatement." [10]

In London Borough of Islington the Tribunal considered Paragraph 84(2) of the Code and stated at [117]:

"it is apparent that the list is not intended to be exhaustive: the power to order compensation "includes power" to order payment for the matters identified. In this case the relevant power is under para.25(1), which, in apparently unrestricted terms, confers jurisdiction to "order the operator to pay compensation to the relevant person for any loss or damage that has been sustained or will be sustained by that person as a result of the exercise of the code right". The reference in para.25 to "any loss or damage", the inclusive list of examples in para.84(2), and the incorporation of only some of the heads of compensation available under s.5 of the Land Compensation Act 1961, all suggest that other types of loss or damage may be capable of being the subject of compensation under para.25. It was however suggested ...that the only right to compensation was under the headings in para.84(2), but our provisional view is that that is too narrow an approach. It is not necessary for us to reach a concluded view on that question in this reference and we therefore prefer to leave it for consideration on an occasion when it can be fully argued."

Legal and Valuation Expenses

In London Borough of Islington it was not disputed that the site provider was entitled to reasonable legal and valuation expenses in connection with agreeing the Code agreement and for the temporary use of its land at ground level for a working compound.

The Tribunal noted that no attempt had been made to quantify the legal and valuation expenses.[11] It accepted that the recoverable fees were those incurred in seeking to agree terms for a code agreement and do not include costs incurred in resisting the agreement in principle or to compromise the reference itself. Those matters were decisions for the

[10] Communications Act 2003, Schedule 3A, Paragraph 84(2).

[11] [2019] UKUT 0053 at [122].

Tribunal as costs of the reference, as made clear by Martin Roger QC in London Borough of Islington at [94]:

"*Where a new letting is imposed by the Upper Tribunal on a reference under the Code the landlord is entitled, as a matter of law, to ask the tribunal to order a payment of compensation equal to its reasonable legal and valuation expenses (para.84(2)(a)). It is to be expected that such compensation will be ordered as a matter of routine, as it is in compulsory purchase cases, and that expectation is the basis of the universal practice concerning contributions to fees on new lettings and renewals. The willing landlord would be aware both of the right and of the practice, in the same way as it would be aware of the basis on which the tribunal would assess a rent. Mr Stott's approach to valuation assumes that the parties would conduct their rent negotiation with a view to mirroring the basis of valuation under the Code, and would therefore reach agreement on a rent reflecting the "no network" assumption. For the same reason the parties would agree that, since no fees are in fact to be paid under the terms they have settled on, an equivalent annual allowance ought to be included in the rent. That allowance, as Mr Jourdan agreed, should be £445.*"

In *Cornerstone Telecommunications Infrastructure Ltd v London & Quadrant Housing Trust* [12] the only compensation payable was the £3,068 reasonable legal expenses in advising on and completing the agreement a sum which did not include the costs incurred in respect of the proceedings. The Tribunal rejected a suggestion by the operator that the sum payable should be £3000 on the basis that there was no reason not to award the sum actually incurred.

Diminution in Value

Paragraph 84(3) of the Code applies *"rules (2) to (4) set out in section 5 of the Land Compensation Act 1961"* for the purpose of assessing diminution in value of the land in relation to England and Wales, which provide as follows:

[12] [2020] UKUT 0282 (LC).

"*(2) The value of land shall, subject as hereinafter provided, be taken to be the amount which the land if sold in the open market by a willing seller might be expected to realise.*

(2A) The value of land referred to in rule (2) is to be assessed in the light of the no-scheme principle set out in section 6A.

(3) The special suitability or adaptability of the land for any purpose shall not be taken into account if that purpose is a purpose to which it could be applied only in pursuance of statutory powers, or for which there is no market apart from the requirements of any authority possessing compulsory purchase powers.

(4) Where the value of the land is increased by reason of the use thereof or of any premises thereon in a manner which could be restrained by any court, or is contrary to law, or is detrimental to the health of the occupants of the premises or to the public health, the amount of that increase shall not be taken into account."

There is a contrast between the assessment of consideration [13] and compensation because the assumptions and disregards under Paragraph 24 of the Code do not apply when assessing compensation under Paragraphs 25(1) and 84(2)(b) of the Code.

In *London Borough of Islington*, the Tribunal considered that the policy of a reduction of costs in providing high quality telecommunications service was apparent in the no-network assumption in Paragraph 24, but was not a policy which had the same impact in relation to the assessment of compensation.[14] However, the Tribunal also considered that it was not Parliament's intention to give the economic value that had been denied under the new consideration scheme in the form of compensation for diminution in value of the land.[15] The Tribunal noted that there was a distinction between compensation for diminution in the value of the land

[13] For which, see Chapter 6.

[14] [2019] UKUT 0053 at [130].

[15] Ibid, at [131].

and consideration.[16] Consideration is a one-off periodic payment for grant of the right, while compensation was:

"recompense for loss or damage suffered by the site provider as a consequence of the agreement reached or imposed; it is the monetary equivalent of the loss or damage sustained. A site provider which allows its land to be occupied and which receives in return the market value of that occupation on a periodic basis does not suffer loss or damage from being kept out of the use of the land or from being deprived of the opportunity to let it to someone else."[17]

The Tribunal acknowledged that the valuation assumptions prevented the site provider from realising recovering the true value of the land, and that this did not give rise to a loss for which compensation was payable under Paragraph 84 of the Code and did not, without more, give rise to loss or damage.[18] The Tribunal considered that the diminution in the value of the land was capable of being reflected in the consideration payable under Paragraph 24 of the Code. However, it was accepted that if it could be shown that the value of the land had been diminished to a greater extent than had been reflected in the assessment of consideration a separate claim may be admissible.[19]

Finally, the Tribunal noted that there could be circumstances in which the fact that the rights were to be used for the purpose of the electronic communications network (a factor disregarded in assessing compensation) could lead to a diminution in the value of the land. Further, circumstances occurring at a later date may result in an additional loss which was not anticipated when consideration was assessed which it was considered likely to be admissible in principle.[20]

Other Claims for Compensation

In *London Borough of Islington*, the Council put forward 29 separate claims for compensation on a variety of bases. This included 16 claims where a disturbance might be caused. The Tribunal rejected all of the

[16] Ibid, at [132]

[17] Ibid.

[18] Ibid, at [133].

[19] Ibid, at [134].

[20] Ibid at [135].

claims for compensation save for the claims for legal and surveying costs and damage flowing from the installation of the apparatus.[21] A number of the claims were regarded as double counting because they were matters in respect of which consideration was payable, and others were unnecessary because they were already dealt with under the terms of the imposed agreement or dispute resolution provisions.[22]

Evidence for Compensation Claims

The quality of the evidence of loss will be of critical importance to the Tribunal. The valuation evidence in *London Borough of Islington* was described by the Tribunal in *London & Quadrant Housing Trust* as having been "*rudimentary*" as compared with the more detailed evidence in *Vodafone Ltd v Hanover Capital Ltd*[23] in which there was evidence of the behaviour of professionally advised parties negotiating in the real market, and in which it was apparent where the no-network assumption had been taken into account. The Tribunal emphasised that "*the loss and damage anticipated in any particular case will depend on the characteristics of the particular site.*"[24] The site provider should be prepared to adduce expert evidence and pertinent evidence of specific losses.

Summary

In summary:

(1) Where there is an agreement to confer rights under the Code by consent under Part 2, the Tribunal has no power to order compensation under Paragraph 84 of the Code;

(2) Under Paragraph 25 of the Code, the power of the Tribunal to award compensation is dependent upon an order being made by Paragraph 20, and Part 14 of the Code applies if the power of the Tribunal is

[21] See ibid, at [136]-[144].

[22] The position in relation to the claims was prepared prior to the final terms of the agreement being known and so the position regarding double counting and unnecessary terms were largely as a result of this and acknowledged in written submissions.

[23] [2021] 2 P&CR 3.

[24] [2020] UKUT 0282 (LC) at [102].

exercised pursuant to Paragraph 25 or where exercised in relation to Paragraph 44(5) for removal of apparatus;

(3) When the Tribunal has power to make an order for compensation, that power is flexible but not discretionary providing loss and damage has been sustained;

(4) An order for compensation may specify the amount or give directions for determination of the amount including a direction for the dispute about quantum to be agreed or referred to arbitration;

(5) There is no restriction on when compensation can be ordered if the power to compensate is triggered;

(6) The operator may not be subject to a claim for compensation save under the Code, providing it is lawfully exercising its rights;

(7) Double recovery is impermissible. If a matter is taken into account in relation to consideration it may not also be the subject of an award of compensation;

(8) The heads of compensation include reasonable legal and valuation expenses, which will not include the costs of proceedings in the Tribunal;[25]

(9) Compensation will include diminution in value of the land unless already reflected in the consideration payable; and

(10) Any other matters which were already addressed under the terms of the agreement, or dispute resolution mechanism, will not be taken into account.

---

[25] For which, see Chapter 13.

CHAPTER EIGHT

PART 5 OF THE CODE, AND THE CONTINUATION AND TERMINATION OF CODE AGREEMENTS TO WHICH IT APPLIES

In this chapter we address:

(1) The application of Part 5 of the Code;

(2) The continuation of code agreements to which Part 5 of the Code applies; and

(3) The termination of code agreements, to which Part 5 of the Code applies, by –

(a) Site provider giving notice under Paragraph 30 of the Code,

(b) Code operators, and

(c) Consent.

The Application of Part 5 of the Code

Paragraph 28 of the Code explains that Part 5 deals with:

"(a) the continuation of rights after the time at which they cease to be exercisable under an agreement,

(b) the procedure for bringing an agreement to an end,

(c) the procedure for changing an agreement relating to code rights, and

(d) the arrangements for the making of payments under an agreement whilst disputes under this Part are resolved."

The matters referred to in Paragraphs 28(a) and (b) of the Code are dealt with below in this chapter, whereas Paragraphs 28(c) and (d) of the Code are considered in Chapter 9.

Pursuant to Paragraph 29(1) of the Code, Part 5 applies to *"an agreement under Part 2 of this code"*[1] subject to Paragraphs 29(2) to (4).[2] These sub-paragraphs in turn provide that Part 5 of the Code does not apply to a lease of land in England and Wales if its primary purpose is not to grant code rights and is one to which Part 2 of the 1954 Act:[3]

(1) Applies, granting security of tenure for business, professional and other tenants;[4] or

(2) Does not apply and so does not confer security of tenure, but only by virtue of an agreement to exclude that security entered into pursuant to Section 38A of the 1954 Act.[5]

These provisions are then complemented by the newly added Section 43(4) of the 1954 Act:

"This Part does not apply to a tenancy–

(a) the primary purpose of which is to grant code rights within the meaning of Schedule 3A to the Communications Act 2003 (the electronic communications code), and

(b) which is granted after that Schedule comes into force."

The purpose of Paragraph 29 of the Code and Section 43(4) of the 1954 Act together is to prevent, when a code agreement in the form of a lease comes to an end, code operators from being able to choose between which regime they wish to renew their code rights under (the Code or

[1] The reason why Part 2 of the Code is specified here does not become immediately apparent until after one has read the transitional provisions, for which see Chapter 12. In essence, it is because Part 5 of the Code is capable of applying to some agreements entered into both under the Code and the Old Code.

[2] Sub-paragraph (4) is not considered here as it relates only to leases of land in Northern Ireland.

[3] Landlord and Tenant Act 1954.

[4] Communications Act 2003, Schedule 3A, Paragraph 29(2).

[5] Ibid, Paragraph 29(3).

Part 2 of the 1954 Act) – they will only have the benefit of one regime. This was done to remedy an injustice that existed under the Old Code, by which code operators with 1954 Act-protected tenancies that conferred code rights could choose to renew under one or other of the schemes, depending on which was more advantageous to them in all the circumstances.

The Continuation of Code Rights

Pursuant to Paragraph 30(2) of the Code,[6] where a code right is binding on a person (the *"site provider"*) as the result of a code agreement, and under the terms of that code agreement either the code right ceases to be exercisable, the site provider ceases to be bound by it or, the site provider may bring the code agreement to an end so far as it relates to the code right in question:[7]

"the code agreement continues so that–

(a) the operator may continue to exercise that right, and

(b) the site provider continues to be bound by the right." [8]

Paragraph 30(2) of the Code is designed to prevent code agreements, and the code rights conferred thereunder, from being brought to an end by effluxion of time, or some other mechanism contained in the terms of the code agreement (in the case of a code agreement in the form of a lease, this could be by forfeiture).

Once a code right continues to be exercisable by the code operator solely by virtue of Paragraph 30(2) of the Code, only then does it become possible for site providers to seek to terminate the code right under Paragraph 31 of the Code (which is considered below), or for both site

[6] Which is contained in Part 5, and so does not apply the forms of lease specified in Paragraphs 29(2) to (4) of the Code.

[7] Communications Act 2003, Schedule 3A, Paragraph 30(1).

[8] Ibid, Paragraph 30(2).

providers and code operators to seek to vary the terms of the code agreement under Paragraph 33 of the Code.[9]

It is important to note that, pursuant to Paragraph 30(3) of the Code, Paragraph 30(2) of the Code does not apply to interim or temporary code rights.

The Termination of Code Agreements to Which Part 5 of the Code Applies

By the Site Provider

Pursuant to Paragraph 31 of the Code,[10] a site provider who is a party to a code agreement can give notice to the code operator to terminate the code agreement.[11]

A notice under Paragraph 30 of the Code must:

"(a) comply with paragraph 89 (notices given by persons other than operators),

(b) specify the date on which the site provider proposes the code agreement should come to an end, and

(c) state the ground on which the site provider proposes to bring the code agreement to an end."[12]

The requirements of Paragraph 89 of the Code are set out in Chapter 3.

Paragraph 31(3) provides that the date specified in the notice must fall:

"(a) after the end of the period of 18 months beginning with the day on which the notice is given, and

(b) after the time at which, apart from paragraph 30, the code right to which the agreement relates would have ceased to be exercisable or to bind the

[9] See ibid, Paragraphs 31(3)(b) and 33(3)(b). See Chapter 9 for variation of code agreements under Part 5.

[10] Which is contained in Part 5, and so does not apply the forms of lease specified in Paragraphs 29(2) to (4) of the Code.

[11] Ibid, Paragraph 31(1).

[12] Ibid, Paragraph 31(2)

site provider or at a time when, apart from that paragraph, the code agreement could have been brought to an end by the site provider." [13]

The interpretation of Paragraph 31(3) of the Code was central to *EE Ltd and Hutchison 3G UK Ltd v Edelwind Ltd and the Secretary of State for Housing, Communities and Local Government*.[14] The relevant facts are as follows:

(1) EE Ltd ("**EE**") acquired the right by a code agreement ("**Agreement 1**") under the Old Code to install and operate telecoms equipment on a rooftop site until 29 November 2024 from the Secretary of State for Housing, Communities and Local Government ("**S**"), the leaseholder of the site;

(2) At the same time, EE entered into an agreement ("**Agreement 2**") with both S and Edelwind Ltd ("**Edelwind**"), the freeholder of the site, in which Edelwind agreed to be bound by the terms of Agreement 1;

(3) In 2010, EE sought to assign Agreements 1 and 2 to itself and Hutchison 3G UK Ltd ("**H3G**"), another code operator;

(4) On 14 December 2018, Edelwind exercised a break clause in its lease with S, which would bring S's lease of the site to an end on 2 April 2021

(5) In December 2019, S and Edelwind served notices on both EE and H3G under Paragraph 31 of the Code, seeking to end the agreement conferring code rights (without specific reference to either Agreement 1 or Agreement 2) on dates after 21 April 2021; and

(5) EE and H3G challenged the validity of the notices given under Paragraph 31 of the Code, as they claimed that, *inter alia*, neither S nor Edelwind could serve any notice under Paragraph 31 of the Code until after 29 November 2024.

The Tribunal found that, by virtue of the fact that S's lease would come to an end on 2 April 2021 by virtue of Edelwind's exercise of its break

[13] Ibid, Paragraph 31(3).

[14] [2020] 9 WLUK 223.

clause, Agreement 1 would similarly come to an end on 2 April 2021 and thereafter continue under Paragraph 30(2) of the Code.[15] As the terms of Agreement 2 merely provided that Edelwind be bound by the terms of Agreement 1, Agreement 2 would similarly come to an end on 2 April 2021 and continue in the same vein thereafter.[16]

Paragraph 31(3) does not require that any notice given thereunder be given on a date after the relevant code agreement has begun to continue by virtue of Paragraph 30(2) of the Code. It only requires that eighteen months' notice be given, and the termination date be a date after the relevant code agreement has begun to continue by virtue of Paragraph 30(2) of the Code. As a result, the notices given to EE were valid.[17] As these proceedings concerned the validity of the notices, the Tribunal did not determine whether any of the relevant grounds were made out.

The four potential grounds set out in Paragraph 31(4) are:

"(a) that the code agreement ought to come to an end as a result of substantial breaches by the operator of its obligations under the agreement;

(b) that the code agreement ought to come to an end because of persistent delays by the operator in making payments to the site provider under the agreement;

(c) that the site provider intends to redevelop all or part of the land to which the code agreement relates, or any neighbouring land, and could not reasonably do so unless the code agreement comes to an end;

(d) that the operator is not entitled to the code agreement because the test under paragraph 21 for the imposition of the agreement on the site provider is not met."[18]

The first two grounds relate to breach of the terms of the code agreement; the site provider should not be compelled to remain party to a contract that the code operator does not honour. The second two grounds

[15] Ibid, at [38].

[16] Ibid, at [49].

[17] The notices given to H3G were not effective, as the Tribunal determined that EE's attempt to assign each Agreements 1 and 2 to itself and H3G in 2010 were ineffective.

[18] Ibid, Paragraph 31(4).

replicate both the redevelopment defence and the general test for the imposition of a code agreement present in Paragraph 21 of the Code.[19]

Following service of a notice under Paragraph 31 of the Code, Paragraph 32 provides for what happens next. The code agreement will come to an end on the date stated in the notice, unless the code operator either:

"(a) within the period of three months beginning with the day on which the notice is given… gives the site provider a counter-notice in accordance with sub-paragraph (3), and

(b) within the period of three months beginning with the day on which the counter-notice is given, the operator applies to the court for an order under paragraph 34." [20]

Together with complying with Paragraph 88 of the Code,[21] the counter-notice must state:

"(a) that the operator does not want the existing code agreement to come to an end,

(b) that the operator wants the site provider to agree to confer or be otherwise bound by the existing code right on new terms, or

(c) that the code operator wants the site provider to agree to confer or be otherwise bound by a new code right in place of the existing code right." [22]

Whereas Sub-paragraph 32(3)(a) of the Code allows the code operator to simply oppose an attempt by the site provider to terminate the existing code agreement, Sub-paragraphs 32(3)(b) and (c) of the Code allow the code operator to instead seek to vary their existing contractual relationship by way of its counter-notice, instead of having to serve a separate notice under Paragraph 33 of the Code. The parties' ability to seek variation of code agreements is considered in Chapter 9.

---

[19] For which see Chapter 4.

[20] Communications Act 2003, Schedule 3A, Paragraph 32(1).

[21] For which see Chapter 3.

[22] Communications Act 2003, Schedule 3A, Paragraph 32(3).

Importantly, the time limits and consequences set out in Paragraph 32(1) of the Code do not apply in the event that the code operator and site provider agree to the continuation of the extant code agreement.[23]

Where no agreement is reached between the parties, and the code operator serves its counter-notice and then applies under Paragraph 34 of the Code:

"(4) If... the court decides that the site provider has established any of the grounds stated in the site provider's notice under paragraph 31, the court must order that the code agreement comes to an end in accordance with the order.

(5) Otherwise the court must make one of the orders specified in paragraph 34."[24]

In the event that the site provider fails to make out one of the grounds contained in its notice, and the code operator's counter-notice relied upon Paragraph 32(3)(a) of the Code (stating that it does not want the existing code agreement to come to an end), the Tribunal will most likely make an order pursuant to Paragraph 34(2) of the Code:

"that the operator may continue to exercise the existing code right in accordance with the existing code agreement for such period as may be specified in the order (so that the code agreement has effect accordingly)."

Other potential orders that can be made under Paragraph 34 of the Code (including where the counter-notice relies upon Paragraph 32(3)(b) or (c) of the Code) are considered in Chapter 9.

By the Code Operator

Curiously, Paragraph 31(1) of the Code provides only that site providers can serve notices on code operators seeking to bring code agreements to an end; not the other way around. In fact, the Code does not provide any express machinery through which a code operator can seek to terminate

[23] Ibid, Paragraph 32(2).

[24] Ibid, Paragraph 32(4) and (5).

a code agreement to which Part 5 of the Code applies (other than in the context of a novation under Paragraph 33 of the Code).[25]

Given that Paragraph 30(1) of the Code provides that a code agreement will continue in any circumstances where a code right ceases to be exercisable under the code agreement, it likely follows that a break clause (or other contractually-provided means of termination) exercised by a code operator will not be effective to terminate the code agreement.

As set out in Chapter 2, Paragraph 3 of the Code provides that a *"code right"* is *"a right for the statutory purposes"* set out therein. It is therefore conceivable that if, by the effective date of a break notice given by a code operator under a code agreement, the code operator has vacated the site, removed its telecoms apparatus, and so no longer exercises its code right for any of the statutory purposes set out in Paragraph 3 of the Code, then the code agreement will not continue under Paragraph 30(1) of the Code because the relevant right is no longer a code right, and Paragraph 30(1) of the Code only takes effect to continue code agreements that confer code rights.

Under those circumstances it might be possible for a code operator to effectively terminate a code agreement by giving notice. However, unless and until there is a reported case on this issue, whether or not a code operator is capable of effectively terminating a code agreement (in the circumstances set out above, or any others that may operate similarly) remains uncertain.

<u>By Consent</u>

A similar issue arises in the context of whether a code operator and site provider can agree to a surrender of a code agreement to which Part 5 of the Code applies by consent that avoids Paragraph 30(2) of the Code taking effect to continue the code agreement.

Paragraph 30(1)(b) of the Code provides that the code agreement will continue where the code right ceases to be exercisable, the site provider ceases to be bound by it or, the site provider may bring the code

[25] For which, see Chapter 9.

agreement to an end so far as it relates to the code right in question *"under the terms of the agreement"*.

In theory, a surrender of a code agreement that is not achieved pursuant to exercise of contractual terms set out in the code agreement itself does not take effect *"under the terms of the* [code] *agreement"* in question.

Again, whether or not such a surrender would be effective to terminate a code agreement remains uncertain pending authority on the subject.

Summary

In summary:

(1) Part 5 of the Code, which covers continuation, termination and modification of code agreements applies to all agreements falling under Part 2 of the Code, except where the code agreement is a lease and the primary purpose of the lease is not to grant code rights, or is one to which the 1954 Act applies (or which does not apply because of an agreement to exclude that security as provided under Section 38A of the 1954 Act);

(2) Code agreements to which Part 5 of the code applies will continue under Paragraph 30(2) of the Code, notwithstanding that the terms of the code agreement may provide for their earlier termination;

(3) Site providers can seek to terminate code agreements to which Part 5 of the Code applies on a date after the code agreement has begun to continue under Paragraph 30(2) of the Code by giving eighteen months' notice to the code operator and relying on one of four grounds. The code agreement will then terminate unless the code operator gives a counter- notice and subsequently applies to the Tribunal for either an order that the code agreement continue on the same terms, or be varied. The Tribunal will terminate the code agreement if one of the grounds is made out. If not, the Tribunal may make other orders under Paragraph 34 of the Code;

(4) It is conceivable, but not certain, that a code operator can exercise a break clause in a code agreement to which Part 5 of the Code applies, in order to terminate a code agreement and evade Paragraph 30(2) of the Code, provided that it has ceased to use the code right for one of

the statutory purposes set out in Paragraph 3 of the Code by the date specified in the break notice; and

(5) It is conceivable, but not certain, that the site provider and code operator can terminate a code agreement to which Part 5 of the Code applies by consent by effective a surrender, provided that surrender is not achieved pursuant to terms set out in the code agreement.

CHAPTER NINE

VARIATION OF CODE AGREEMENTS, AND INTERIM PAYMENTS OF CONSIDERATION

In this chapter we address:

(1) The procedure for variation of code agreements to which Part 5 of the Code applies;

(2) The orders that can be made by the Tribunal in an application to modify a code agreement under Part 5 of the Code; and

(3) Interim payments of consideration pending applications to terminate or vary code agreements under Part 5 of the Code.

The Procedure for Varying the Terms of a Code Agreement

By the Code Operator's Counter-Notice under Paragraph 32(3)(b) or (c)

As set out in Chapter 8, a code operator may respond to a termination notice given to it by the *"site provider"* under Paragraph 33 of the Code by with a counter-notice under Paragraph 32.

The code operator may respond under Sub-paragraph 32(3)(a) of the Code, stating that it does not want the code agreement to come to an end, or the code operator can state under Sub-paragraph 32(3)(b) or (c) that it either wants the site provider to agree to confer or be otherwise bound by:

(1) The existing code right on new terms;[1] or

(2) A new code right in place of the existing code right.[2]

---

[1] Communications Act 2003, Schedule 3A, Paragraph 32(3)(a).

[2] Ibid, Paragraph 32(3)(b).

Pursuant to Paragraph 32(5) of the Code, if the site provider is unable to make out any of the grounds contained in its termination notice *"the court must make one of the orders specified in paragraph 34"*, which are considered in more detail below.

<u>By Either Party under Paragraph 33</u>

The procedure for a change to the terms of a code agreement, to which Part 5 of the Code applies, that either of the parties to the code agreement (that is both the site provider and operator) may utilise is set out at Paragraph 33 of the Code. Either party may, by notice that complies with the provisions of Paragraph 33(1), require the other party to agree that that:

"*(a) the code agreement should have effect with modified terms,*

(b) where under the code agreement more than one code right is conferred by or otherwise binds the site provider, that the agreement should no longer provide for an existing code right to be conferred by or otherwise bind the site provider,

(c) the code agreement should—

(i) confer an additional code right on the operator, or

(ii) provide that the site provider is otherwise bound by an additional code right, or

(d) the existing code agreement should be terminated and a new agreement should have effect between the parties which—

(i) confers a code right on the operator, or

(ii) provides for a code right to bind the site provider."

Paragraph 33(2)(a) of the Code provides that any notice given under Paragraph 33(1) must comply with either Paragraph 88 or 89 of the Code, depending on whether the notice is given by the operator or site provider.[3] Further, pursuant to Paragraph 33(2)(b), the notice must specify:

[3] For which, see Chapter 3.

"(i) the day from which it is proposed the modified terms should have effect,

(ii) the day from which the agreement should no longer provide for the code right to be conferred by or bind the site provider,

(iii) the day from which it is proposed that the additional code right should be conferred by or otherwise bind the site provider, or

(iv) the day on which it is proposed the existing code agreement should be terminated and from which the new agreement should have effect,

(as the case may be)"

Paragraph 33(2)(c) of the Code contains further requirements for the notice to set out the details of:

"(i) the proposed modified terms,

(ii) the code right it is proposed should no longer be conferred by or otherwise bind the site provider,

(iii) the proposed additional code right, or

(iv) the proposed terms of the agreement,

(as the case may be)."

Similar to termination notices, Paragraph 33(3) of the Code provides that the day specified in accordance with Paragraph 33(2)(b) must be:

(1) After the end of six months starting from the date the notice is given (twelve months shorter than for termination notices); and

(2) On a date after the code agreement has begun to continue under Paragraph 30(2) of the Code.[4]

Paragraph 33(4) and (5) of the Code provide that, in the event that agreement on the proposal in the notice is not reached within six months

[4] For which, see Chapter 8.

commencing on the day the notice is given, either party may apply for an order under Paragraph 34.[5]

The Orders the Tribunal May Make

Paragraph 34 of the Code specifies the orders that the Tribunal may make on an application under Paragraph 32(1)(b) or Paragraph 33(5) of the Code. The powers conferred on the Tribunal are broad.

The powers include, by Paragraph 34(2) of the Code, continuation of the existing right in accordance with the existing agreement for a period specified in the order. This is likely to be used either where a site provider has failed to make out any of the grounds contained in its termination notice, or on an application to vary the terms of the code agreement where neither party is able to persuade the Tribunal to make any of the other available orders.

The Tribunal may modify the terms relating to the existing code right under Paragraph 34(3) of the Code. If more than one code right is conferred under the agreement, Paragraph 34(4) of the Code empowers the Tribunal to modify the code agreement so that it no longer provides for one or more code rights to bind the site provider (provided at least one code right in the original code agreement remains conferred or binding thereunder). Further, by Paragraph 34(5) of the Code, the Tribunal may modify the agreement to confer an additional code right on the operator, or to provide that the site provider is otherwise bound by an additional code right.

Paragraph 34(6) of the Code empowers the Tribunal to vary the code agreement by novation:

"The court may order the termination of the code agreement relating to the existing right and order the operator and the site provider to enter into a new agreement which–

(a) confers a code right on the operator, or

---

[5] It does not appear that it is only the person that gave the notice that may apply. The wording of Paragraph 33(4) is wide enough to permit either the party who serves or receives the notice to make the application to the Tribunal.

(b) provides for a code right to bind the site provider."

The existing code agreement will continue until the new agreement takes effect,[6] and the Code applies to the new agreement as if it were an agreement under Part 2 of the Code.[7]

Paragraph 34(9) of the Code provides that the terms providing for the new code right are to be agreed between the operator and site provider. If terms cannot be agreed, either party may apply to the Tribunal which will then impose those terms,[8] and in such a case the Tribunal is also required to have regard to the terms of the existing code agreement.[9]

Paragraph 34(11) of the Code provides that Paragraphs 23(2) to (8) (which relate to the terms of an agreement),[10] Paragraph 24 (how consideration is to be determined),[11] Paragraph 25 (rights to the payment of compensation) and Paragraph 84 (compensation under the Code) [12] apply to an order under Sub-paragraphs (3), (4) and (5) so far as it modifies or specifies the terms of the agreement, and to an order under Sub-paragraph (1), just as they apply to an order under Paragraph 20 of the Code.

Paragraph 34(13) of the Code requires the Tribunal to have regard to all the circumstances of the case in deciding what order to make. Certain circumstances are specified as being matters which must, in particular be considered. These matters are:

"(a) the operator's business and technical needs,

(b) the use that the site provider is making of the land to which the existing code agreement relates,

(c) any duties imposed on the site provider by an enactment, and

---

[6] Communications Act 2003, Schedule 3A, Paragraph 34(7).

[7] Ibid, Paragraph 34(8).

[8] Ibid, Paragraph 34(10).

[9] Ibid, Paragraph 34(12).

[10] For which, see Chapter 5.

[11] See Chapter 6.

[12] See Chapter 7.

(d) the amount of consideration payable by the operator to the site provider under the existing code agreement."

Where an order is made pursuant to Paragraph 34 of the Code, the Tribunal has power under Paragraph 34(14) to direct the code operator to pay the site provider the amount (if any) by which A exceeds B in which:

"*(a) A is the amount of consideration that would have been payable by the operator to the site provider for the relevant period if that amount had been assessed on the same basis as the consideration payable as the result of the order, and*

(b) B is the amount of consideration payable by the operator to the site provider for the relevant period."

And the *"relevant period"* for the purpose of Paragraph 34(14) of the Code is defined in Paragraph 34(15) as the period (if any) that:

"*(a) begins on the date on which, apart from the operation of paragraph 30, the code right to which the existing code agreement relates would have ceased to be exercisable or to bind the site provider or from which, apart from that paragraph, the code agreement could have been brought to an end by the site provider, and*

(b) ends on the date on which the order is made."

The exercise of Tribunal's powers to make orders under Paragraph 34 was recently considered as a preliminary issue by the President of the Tribunal, Mr Justice Fancourt, in *EE Ltd and Hutchison 3G UK Ltd v Stephenson and AP Wireless (II) UK Ltd*.[13] In that case, following the expiry of a lease that was a subsisting agreement to which Part 5 of the Code applied,[14] the code operator served the site provider with a notice under Paragraph 33(1)(d) of the Code seeking that the parties enter into a new agreement to confer a code right at a considerably lower rent.

The parties were unable to reach agreement within six months, so the code operator applied under Paragraph 33(5) of the Code for an order

13 [2021] UKUT 167 (LC).

14 For which, see Chapter 12.

under Paragraph 34(6). The site provider opposed the application on the basis that, when having regard to all the circumstances of the case and the factors contained at Paragraph 34(13) of the Code, the Tribunal should not make an order under Paragraph 34(6) because the code operator had failed to advance a site-specific need for a novation of the existing agreement. This argument was advanced reliant in part on the principle in *O'May v City of London Real Property Co Ltd*,[15] which provides that in lease renewals under Part 2 of the 1954 Act there is a presumption against change of the terms of the existing agreement, and so a heavy onus lay on the party seeking variation to justify it.

The President initially observed at [46] that *"The Code was intended to confer broader rights and more flexibility on operators, in view of the impending arrival of 5G networks and new technology."* He went on at [47] to explain that whilst Parliament had indeed decided that the Code should not have retrospective effect. *"It cannot have been intended that the public benefits and investments incentives conferred by the new Code would be stultified by the continuation of subsisting agreements, with more limited rights at higher rents or fees, for a significant time after their expiry dates."*

In this context, the President concluded that *"it seems clear that an operator under a subsisting agreement should not have to prove a site-specific justification for the replacement of an expired subsisting agreement with a new Code-compliant agreement. The significant additional rights conferred by the Code, the benefit of some or all of which will have been denied the operator for the duration of the subsisting agreement, are themselves a reason for the grant of a new agreement on different terms."*[16]

The President then considered what it should mean for the Tribunal to have regard to the *"business and technical needs"* of the code operator under Paragraph 34(13)(a) of the Code, and found at [51] that:

---

[15] [1983] 2 AC 726.

[16] It follows that the President's reasoning against a site-specific need for renewal is limited in scope to where agreements entered into under the Old Code are being renewed under the Code. We may see this argument re-surface in the future where a code operator seeks a novation on new terms of an agreement entered into under the Code, and may see a different conclusion reached.

"Parliament cannot have intended to impose on an operator a requirement to prove a specific need for the particular order sought in relation to the site in issue. The business and technical needs of an operator are its reasonable requirements as regards the statutory purposes, namely the provision of its network and an infrastructure system. It seems to me that they may also include a need to have a standard form of agreement for its code agreements, for estate management reasons." [17]

The President held that whilst there were indeed similarities in the wording of Paragraph 34(14) of the Code and Section 35 of the 1954 Act, the provisions were not the same and the purpose underlying the 1954 Act *"was very different"* from the purpose underlying the Code.[18] Instead, *"site providers are required to put up with a degree of change in the public interest of facilitating the provision of a choice of high quality networks."* [19] It followed that the case law under Section 35 of the 1954 Act, including the principle in *O'May*, do not directly apply to orders under Paragraph 34 of the Code.

A second issue arose because the code operator had, in its application under Paragraph 33(5) following service of the notice under Paragraph 33(1)(d) of the Code, sought in the alternative that the Tribunal make a different order under Paragraph 34 of the Code. The site provider argued that this was not permitted, as it was an application for an order varying the extant code agreement that had not been the subject of a prior notice seeking said change.

The President agreed with the site provider and struck out the code operator's application for an alternative order: *"if the notice proposed termination and a new agreement on terms annexed, the giver of the notice cannot apply to the court for modification of the existing agreement on different terms..."* [20] *"it is not permissible for an applicant to plead an*

---

[17] Agreeing with the decision of the Court of Session (Inner House) in *EE Ltd and Hutchinson 3G UK Ltd v Duncan* [2021] CSIH 27.

[18] [2021] UKUT 167 (LC) at [53].

[19] Ibid, at [55].

[20] Ibid, at [63].

alternative case for a different change to the existing agreement unless it has served a notice that identifies the relief sought."[21]

However, the Tribunal went on to explain that it would have been open to the site provider to *"waive any non-compliance if they are content to engage with the application that has been made"*[22] or *"to plead that an order terminating the existing agreement and for a new agreement should not be made because, in the particular circumstances of the case, a different order that the court may make is more appropriate, or is sufficient for the applicant's needs."*[23]

Interim Payments of Consideration

Where there is a pending application by either the code operator or site provider under Paragraph 32(1)(b) or 33(5) of the Code,[24] Paragraph 35 of the Code gives the site provider three options as to how consideration payable under the extant code agreement should be treated in the interim. The site provider may:

(1) Agree with the code operator that they will continue to receive the payments of consideration to which they are entitled under the extant code agreement, until the relevant application has been determined;[25]

(2) Agree with the code operator that it will pay to the site provider different payments of consideration to which they are entitled under the extant code agreement, until the relevant application has been determined;[26] or

(3) Apply to the Tribunal for it to determine what consideration should be payable to the site provider under the extant code agreement until the application has been determined.[27]

---

21 Ibid, at [66].

22 Ibid, at [63].

23 Ibid, at [65].

24 Communications Act 2003, Schedule 3A, Paragraph 35(1).

25 Ibid, Paragraph 35(2)(a).

26 Ibid, Paragraph 35(2)(b).

27 Ibid, Paragraph 35(2)(c).

In the event that the Tribunal is required to determine the consideration to be paid, it will do so in accordance with the basis set out in Paragraph 24 of the Code.[28] This scheme clearly draws inspiration from applications for interim rent under Section 24A of the 1954 Act.

Summary

In summary:

(1) Where a site provider gives a code operator a termination notice, the code operator's counter-notice may seek variation of the code agreement (in the event that the site provider is unable to make out any of the grounds for termination);

(2) Alternatively, either party may serve a notice requiring the other to agree that the code agreement be modified, which can include modification of terms, the removal of rights, the inclusion of additional rights, or a new agreement conferring one or more new code rights;

(3) The notice must comply with the formalities required under Paragraphs 88 or 89 of the Code (as applicable), and must specify the date (no less than six months from the date of the notice, and after the date on which the code agreement began to continue under Paragraph 30(2) of the Code) on which the modified terms, additional or removed code rights, or new agreement shall have effect, and adequate details of the changes;

(4) In the event of no agreement within 6 months of the date notice is given, either party may apply for an order under Paragraph 34 of the Code;

(5) The powers of the Tribunal under the Code are wide ranging and include powers to continue the existing agreement, modify its terms, remove or add code rights, or order that a new agreement conferring new code rights be entered into;

(6) In making an order, the Tribunal is required to consider all the circumstances, but to have particular regard to four factors set out in

---

[28] Ibid, Paragraph 35(3).

Paragraph 34(13). There is not the same presumption against change which applies to renewal under the 1954 Act;

(7) A code operator need not provide a site-specific justification for a variation of the terms of the code agreement;

(8) The provisions relating to consideration and compensation in other Parts of the Code apply to such an order;

(9) The Tribunal has power to direct the operator to pay the site provider an amount of consideration by reference to the formula set out in Paragraph 34(14) of the Code; and

(10) When an application is pending in the Tribunal either for termination or variation of a code agreement, the parties to the code agreement can agree to maintain the same consideration payments, agree to vary them, or require the Tribunal to determine what the consideration payments up until determination of the pending application should have been, in a similar fashion to how interim rent applications under the 1954 Act operate.

CHAPTER TEN

REMOVAL OF APPARATUS

In this chapter we consider the removal of apparatus as provided for in Part 6 of the Code, including:

(1) The means by which a person can discover whether apparatus is on land pursuant to a code right;

(2) The cases in which a landowner has the right to require the removal of electronic communications apparatus or the restoration of land;

(3) The cases in which a landowner or occupier of neighbouring land has the right to require removal of apparatus; and

(4) The means by which a right to require removal of apparatus or restoration of land can be enforced.

The Procedure for Determining Whether Apparatus is on Land Pursuant to a Code Right

Paragraph 39 of the Code enables a landowner or occupier to ascertain whether apparatus is on land pursuant to a code right. The process enables the landowner to serve a notice requiring a code operator to disclose whether:

"(a) the operator owns electronic communications apparatus on, under or over land in which the landowner has an interest or uses such apparatus for the purposes of the operator's network, or

(b) the operator has the benefit of a code right entitling the operator to keep electronic communications apparatus on, under or over land in which the landowner has an interest." [1]

Further rights are conferred by Paragraph 39(2) of the Code, where the landowner or occupier of neighbouring land may by notice require the

[1] Communications Act 2003, Schedule 3A, Paragraph 39(1).

code operator to disclose whether it owns apparatus over land that forms, or but for the apparatus would form, a means of access to the neighbouring land, or uses such apparatus for the purpose of the operator's network, or has a code right entitling it to keep such apparatus on, over or under such land.

Pursuant to Paragraph 39(3) of the Code, any of these notices served must comply with the requirements of Paragraph 89.[2]

By Paragraph 39(5) the code operator must bear the costs of any action taken by the landowner or occupier under Paragraph 40 to enforce the removal of the apparatus providing the conditions in Sub-paragraph (4) are met, namely:

"(a) the operator does not, before the end of the period of three months beginning with the date on which the notice under sub-paragraph (1) or (2) was given, give a notice to the landowner or occupier that—

(i) complies with paragraph 88 (notices given by operators), and

(ii) discloses the information sought by the landowner or occupier,

(b) the landowner or occupier takes action under paragraph 40 to enforce the removal of the apparatus, and

(c) it is subsequently established that—

(i) the operator owns the apparatus or uses it for the purposes of the operator's network, and

(ii) the operator has the benefit of a code right entitling the operator to keep the apparatus on, under or over the land."

The Conditions Required for a Landowner to have the Right to Require Removal of Apparatus

Paragraph 37(1) of the Code explains that a landowner has the right to require the removal of telecoms apparatus "*if and only if*" one or more of certain conditions are met. It follows that if none of the specified

---

2 For which, see Chapter 3.

conditions is met there is no right to require the operator to remove the equipment.

The First Condition

The first condition is set out in Paragraph 37(2) of the Code. This is that the landowner has never since the coming into force of the Code been bound by a code right entitling the code operator to keep apparatus on, under or over the land. This is self-explanatory.

However, this condition is subject to Paragraph 37(4) considered below.

The Second Condition

The second condition is contained in Paragraph 37(3) of the Code. That is that a code right entitling the operator to keep apparatus on, under or over land has come to an end or ceased to bind the landowner in any one of the following four situations:

(1) Pursuant to Paragraph 37(3)(a) of the Code, where interim code rights have expired as provided for at Paragraph 26(7) and (8) of the Code;[3]

(2) Pursuant to Paragraph 37(3)(b) of the Code, where code rights have been terminated under Paragraph 32(1);[4]

(3) Pursuant to Paragraph 37(3)(c) of the Code, where code rights have been terminated by order under Paragraph 32(4),[5] 34(4) or 34(6);[6] and

(4) Pursuant to Paragraph 37(3)(d) of the Code, where *"the right was granted by a lease to which Part 5 of this code does not apply"*[7] and the lease has ceased to bind the landowner.

[3] For which, see Chapter 4.

[4] For which, see Chapter 8.

[5] For which, see Chapter 8.

[6] For which, see Chapter 9.

[7] For which, see Chapter 8.

Excluding Qualification Under the First or Second Conditions

All of the situations specified in each the first condition under Paragraph 37(2) and the second condition as provided in Paragraph 37(3)(a) to (d) are subject to Paragraph 37(4) of the Code. This provides:

"*(4) The landowner does not meet the first or second condition if—*

(a) the land is occupied by a person who—

(i) conferred a code right (which is in force) entitling an operator to keep the apparatus on, under or over the land, or

(ii) is otherwise bound by such a right, and

(b) that code right was not conferred in breach of a covenant enforceable by the landowner."

The Third Condition

The third condition is set out at Paragraph 37(6) of the Code. It addresses the situation where the apparatus is not or is longer required for use within the network. There are three criteria:

"*(a) an operator has the benefit of a code right entitling the operator to keep the apparatus on, under or over the land, but*

(b) the apparatus is not, or is no longer, used for the purposes of the operator's network, and

(c) there is no reasonable likelihood that the apparatus will be used for that purpose."

The Fourth Condition

The fourth condition is provided in Paragraph 37(7) of the Code and is directed towards the status of the code operator. It contains three elements:

"*(a) this code has ceased to apply to a person so that the person is no longer entitled under this code to keep the apparatus on, under or over the land,*

(b) the retention of the apparatus on, under or over the land is not authorised by a scheme contained in an order under section 117, and

(c) there is no other person with a right conferred by or under this code to keep the apparatus on, under or over the land."

The Fifth Condition

The fifth condition is that the apparatus was kept on the land pursuant to a transport right under Part 7 of the Code or a street work right pursuant to Part 8 of the Code, and that right has ceased to be exercisable pursuant to Paragraph 54(9) of the Code (Paragraph 54 of the Code addresses the position if land ceases to be transport land) and there is no other person with a code right to keep the apparatus on, over or under the land.[8]

The Circumstances in which a Landowner or Occupier of Neighbouring Land has the Right to Require Removal of Apparatus

There are two conditions which must be met for a landowner or occupier of any land (described as *"neighbouring land"*) to require the removal of apparatus. The first is set out in Paragraph 38(2) of the Code, namely that the apparatus "*interferes with or obstructs a means of access to or from the neighbouring land.*" By Paragraph 38(3) of the Code, the second condition is that the landowner or occupier of the neighbouring land is not bound by a code right pursuant to Paragraph 3(h) of the Code, which entitles the operator to cause the interference or obstruction.

However, Paragraph 38(4) provides that the landowner of the neighbouring land, who is not the occupier of the land, does not meet the second condition if the land is occupied by a person who conferred a code right which is in force and which entitles the operator to cause the interference or obstruction, or is otherwise bound by such a right unless the code right was conferred in breach of a covenant enforceable by the landowner.

The key case concerning removal of apparatus is *Evolution (Shinfield) LLP and Others v British Telecommunications PLC*.[9] The facts of this case were as follows:

---

[8] These provisions fall outside the scope of this book.

[9] [2019] UKUT 127 (LC)

(1) Evolution (Shinfield) LLP ("**Evolution**"), a property developer, owned a large development site immediately west of a roundabout;

(2) In 2011, the code operator had installed a telecoms cabinet on a footway on the roundabout;

(3) In 2012, Evolution obtained planning consent for a major new housing development which included creating a new exit from the roundabout. That exit was to go straight through the footway where the cabinet was situated. It was not possible to redesign the roundabout to avoid the removal of the cabinet;

(4) C sought an order under Paragraph 40 of the Code for the removal of the cabinet, and the specification of works for said relocation came to nearly £300,000.00; and

(5) The reference to the Tribunal was a dispute regarding who was responsible for paying for the works, but the preliminary issue arose as to whether Evolution could even require the removal.

Evolution relied on the right conferred by Paragraph 38 of the Code, but the code operator argued that this applied only to means of access that were in existence at the time of the installation of the apparatus. Martin Rodger QC dismissed the reference, and held that *"interferes with or obstructs a means of access to or from neighbouring land"* at Paragraph 38 of the Code refers to *"an existing means of access, rather than something potential."* Importantly, the means of access had to be extant at the time the code rights were conferred.

The Tribunal considered that this is consistent with the general scheme of the Code, in particular the circumstances (set out in Paragraph 13(2) of the Code) under which a code operator is permitted to interfere with or obstruct means of access to neighbouring land. The Tribunal considered that Paragraph 38 of the Code was simply the corollary of Paragraph 13 of the Code; Paragraph 38 of the Code is merely the means of enforcing that rights of way that were in place when the apparatus was installed may not be interfered with unless the owner of the right of way is bound by them.

The Procedure for Removal of Apparatus by the Landowner or Occupier

Pursuant to Paragraph 40(1) of the Code, removal of apparatus by the landowner or occupier pursuant to Paragraph 37 and 38 of the Code is exercisable only in accordance with Paragraph 40 of the Code.

<u>The Notice</u>

Removal is triggered by service of a notice by the landowner or occupier pursuant to Paragraph 40(2) of the Code requiring the operator to remove the apparatus and restore the land to the condition it was in prior to the apparatus being situated on, over or under the land. Pursuant to Paragraphs 40(3)(b) and (4) of the Code, the notice must comply with Paragraph 89 of the Code [10] and specify the period within which the operator must complex the works which must be reasonable.

<u>The Position if No Agreement is Reached</u>

If agreement is not reached within twenty-eight days beginning on the date notice was given in relation to the matters listed in Paragraph 40(5) of the Code then, by Paragraph 40(6) of the Code, the landowner or occupier may apply to the Tribunal either for an order under Paragraph 44(1) of the Code (which requires the operator to remove the apparatus) or for an order under Paragraph 44(3) of the Code (enabling the landowner to sell the apparatus).

The matters listed in Paragraph 40(5) about what agreement must be reached in order to avoid the landowner or occupier having the right to apply to the Tribunal are:

"*(a) that the operator will remove the apparatus;*

(b) that the operator will restore the land to its condition before the apparatus was placed on, under or over the land;

(c) the time at which or period within which the apparatus will be removed;

(d) the time at which or period within which the land will be restored."

---

[10] For which, see Chapter 3.

Pursuant to Paragraph 40(7) of the Code:

"If the court makes an order under paragraph 44(1), but the operator does not comply with the agreement imposed on the operator and the landowner or occupier by virtue of paragraph 44(7), the landowner or occupier may make an application to the court for an order under paragraph 44(3)".

However, on an application either by Paragraph 40(6) or (7) of the Code, the Tribunal may not make an order in relation to apparatus if an application under Paragraph 20(3) of the Code has been made in relation to the apparatus and not yet determined.[11]

The nature of the various orders that can be made under Paragraph 44 are considered below.

Third Party Rights to Remove Apparatus

Paragraph 41(1) of the Code provides that the rights of third parties to require removal of apparatus under an enactment other than the Code, or right other than under an enactment, can only be exercised in accordance with Paragraph 41.

By Paragraph 41(2) and (3) the third party may give notice to the operator (in compliance with the notice requirements in Paragraph 89)[12] to remove the apparatus and restore the land within a specified period which must be reasonable.

Pursuant to Paragraph 41(5) of the Code, the operator has the right to serve a counter-notice within twenty-eight days stating either that the third party is not entitled to require the removal of the apparatus, or specifying the steps which it proposes to take to secure a right as against the third party to keep the apparatus on the land.

In the event that the operator has given a counter-notice, the right of the third party to enforce removal of the apparatus may only be exercised pursuant to an order of the Tribunal.[13]

---

[11] For which, see Chapter 4.

[12] For which, see Chapter 3.

[13] Communications Act 2003, Schedule 3A, Paragraph 41(7).

In the event that the code operator gave a counter-notice specifying the steps which it proposes to take to secure a right as against the third party to keep the apparatus on the land, the Tribunal may only make the order under Paragraph 41(7) if satisfied that the operator is not taking those steps or is being unreasonably dilatory in taking them, or that taking those steps has not secured or will not secure the right to keep the apparatus or to reinstall if removed.[14]

Paragraph 41(9) of the Code enables enforcement by the third party by application where it has the right to enforce the removal of the apparatus, either because no counter-notice was given pursuant to Paragraph 41(6) of the Code, or pursuant to a Tribunal order under Paragraph 41(7) of the Code. The third party can apply either for an order for removal of the apparatus under Paragraph 44(1), or enabling it to sell the apparatus under Paragraph 44(3).

Paragraph 41(10) of the Code provides that if an order is made by the Tribunal under Paragraph 44(1) of the Code, but the operator does not comply with the agreement imposed, the third party may make an application to the Tribunal for an order under Paragraph 44(3).

It should be noted that:

(1) An order made on an application under Paragraph 41 need not include provision within Paragraph 44(1)(b) or (3)(d) unless the Tribunal considers it appropriate;[15] and

(2) The right to seek an order under Paragraph 41(9) of the Code is without prejudice to any other method available to the third party for enforcing the removal of the apparatus.[16]

The nature of the various orders that can be made under Paragraph 44 are considered below.

Paragraph 42 of the Code governs the way in which Paragraph 40 of the Code applies when the third parties' right is the right to require the alteration of the apparatus in consequence of the stopping up, closure,

---

[14] Ibid, Paragraph 41(8).

[15] Ibid, Paragraph 41(11).

[16] Ibid, Paragraph 41(12).

change or diversion of a street or road or the extinguishment or alteration of a public right of way.[17]

A Separate Application for the Restoration of Land

Paragraph 43(1) of the Code enables a separate application to be made in the event that the condition of land has been affected by the exercise of a code right, and restoration of the land to the condition does not involve the removal of apparatus. Pursuant to Paragraph 43(2) of the Code, the owner of the freehold estate, the lessee or the occupier each have the right to require the restoration of the land in the event that the person is not bound by a code right.

This is subject to Paragraph 43(3) of the Code, which excludes the right to make an application in cases in which the land is occupied by a person who conferred a code right that is in force, and where that right entitles the operator to affect the condition of the land in the same way as mentioned in Paragraph 43(1), or is otherwise bound by such a right and that right was not conferred in breach of a covenant enforceable by the relevant person.

In cases where the person has the right under Paragraph 43 of the Code, Paragraphs 43(5) an (7) set out that a notice, compliant with Paragraph 89 of the Code,[18] may be given to the code operator that specifies the period of the works, and that such period must be reasonable.

By Paragraphs 43(8) and (9) of the Code, in the event that agreement is not reached within twenty-eight days that the operator will restore the land, and the time within which the land will be restored, the person may apply to the Tribunal for an order pursuant to Paragraph 44(2) of the Code requiring restoration, or enabling it to recover the cost of restoration. If the code operator does not comply with an order under Paragraph 44(2) of the Code, the person may make an application for an order under Paragraph 44(4) of the Code.[19]

---

[17] A detailed consideration of these provisions is outside the scope of this book.

[18] For which, see Chapter 3.

[19] Communications Act 2003, Schedule 3A, Paragraph 44(10).

The nature of the various orders that can be made under Paragraph 44 are considered next.

Orders on Applications under Paragraphs 40 to 43 of the Code

Paragraph 44 specifies the orders which may be made by the Tribunal on an application under Paragraphs 40 to 43 of the Code.

Any order made under Paragraph 44(1) of the Code is an order that the code operator must, within the period specified in the order:

"(a) remove the electronic communication apparatus, and

(b) restore the land to its condition before the apparatus was placed on, under or over the land." [20]

Paragraph 44(2) of the Code confers the power to make an order that the operator must, within the period specified, restore the land to the condition it was in prior to the installation of the apparatus.

Paragraph 44(3) of the Code provides for an order that the landowner, occupier or third party may:

"(a) remove or arrange the removal of the electronic communications apparatus;

(b) sell any apparatus so removed;

(c) recover the costs of any action under paragraph (a) or (b) from the operator;

(d) recover from the operator the costs of restoring the land to its condition before the apparatus was placed on, under or over the land;

(e) retain the proceeds of sale of the apparatus to the extent that these do not exceed the costs incurred by the landowner, occupier or third party as mentioned in paragraph (c) or (d)."

Orders under Paragraph 44(4) of the Code require that the landowner may recover from the operator the costs of restoring the land to its condition before the code right was exercised.

---

[20] Ibid, Paragraph 44(1).

Paragraph 44(5) of the Code sets out that, on an application under Paragraph 40, the code operator may be ordered to pay compensation to the landowner for any loss or damage suffered by the landowner as a result of the presence of the apparatus on the land during the period when the landowner had the right to require removal of the apparatus but was not able to exercise that right. Paragraph 44(6) provides that further provision about this compensation is made under Paragraph 84(5).

Paragraph 44(7) specifies that an order under either Paragraph 44(1) or (2) takes effect as an agreement between the code operator and the landowner, occupier or third party that requires the code operator to take the steps specified in the order, and otherwise contains such terms as the Tribunal may so specify.

Summary

In summary:

(1) Paragraph 39 of the Code enables a landowner or occupier to ascertain whether apparatus is on land pursuant to a code right, and a landowner or occupier of neighbouring land may by notice require the code operator to disclose whether it owns apparatus over land;

(2) A landowner has the right to require the removal of electronic communications apparatus "*if and only if*" one or more of certain conditions are met as specified in Paragraph 37 of the Code;

(3) Paragraph 38 of the Code provides for the circumstances in which a landowner or occupier of any land can require the removal of apparatus. It refers to apparatus that *"interferes with or obstructs a means of access to or from neighbouring land"*, which the Tribunal has determined refers to an extant, rather than potential or future, means of access. Importantly, the means of access must be extant at the time the Code Rights were conferred;

(4) The procedure for removal of apparatus is specified in Paragraph 40 of the Code and is triggered by service of a notice. If no agreement is reached within twenty-eight days of a notice being served, the landowner or occupier may apply to the Tribunal either for an order under Paragraph 44(1) of the Code, requiring the operator to remove

the apparatus, or for an order under Paragraph 44(3) of the Code enabling the landowner to sell the apparatus;

(5) On an application either by Paragraph 40(6) or (7) of the Code, the Tribunal may not make an order in relation to apparatus if an application under Paragraph 20(3) of the Code has been made in relation to the apparatus and is not yet determined;

(6) Paragraph 41 provides for the rights of third parties to require removal of apparatus in limited circumstances. Again, the procedure is by notice and the code operator has the right to serve a counter-notice within twenty-eight days stating either that the third party is not entitled to require the removal of the apparatus, or specifying the steps which it proposes to take to secure a right as against the third party to keep the apparatus on the land. In the event that the operator has given a counter-notice, the right of the third party to enforce removal of the apparatus may only be pursuant to an order of the Tribunal;

(7) Paragraph 43 of the Code enables a separate application to be made in the event that the condition of land has been affected by the exercise of a code right, and restoration of the land to the condition does not involve the removal of apparatus; and

(8) The Tribunal has wide powers pursuant to Paragraph 44 of the Code on any application under Paragraphs 40 to 43 of the Code requiring the operator to remove the apparatus and restore the land if the conditions are met. There is also power to direct that the landowner, occupier or third party may recover costs of taking such steps. Compensation may be ordered.

CHAPTER ELEVEN

THIRD PARTIES, CODE RIGHTS AND LAND REGISTRATION, AND THE ASSIGNMENT OF CODE RIGHTS

This chapter considers the following:

(1) Which third parties may be bound by code rights granted by others;

(2) How code rights interact with the Land Registration Act 2002 ("**the 2002 Act**"); and

(3) Code operators' ability to assign their code rights to third party operators.

Third Parties who can be Bound by Code Rights

Paragraph 10 of the Code takes effect where:

"a code right is conferred on an operator in respect of land by a person ("O") who is the occupier of the land when the code right is conferred." [1]

In those circumstances, there is a first class of third parties who are automatically bound by the code rights granted by O without the code operator having to take any further steps. These persons are set out in Paragraph 10(2):

"If O has an interest in the land when the code right is conferred, the code right also binds—

(a) successors in title to that interest,

[1] Communications Act 2003, Schedule 3A, Paragraph 10(1).

(b) a person with an interest in the land that is created after the right is conferred and is derived (directly or indirectly) out of—

(i) O's interest, or

(ii) the interest of a successor in title to O's interest, and

(c) any other person at any time in occupation of the land whose right to occupation was granted by—

(i) O, at a time when O was bound by the code right, or

(ii) a person within paragraph (a) or (b)."[2]

And in respect of successors in title bound by a code right under Paragraph 10(2)(a), they are *"to be treated as a party to the agreement by which O conferred the right."*[3]

So, if O is the freehold owner of the land in question:

(1) O's (for example) assigns will be bound, and will be treated as a party to O's code agreement;

(2) If O (or O's assigns) grant a lease of the land to a third party, that lessee will be bound; and

(3) If O (or O's assigns) grant a licence to occupy the land to a third party, that licensee will be bound.

There is then a second class of third parties who are not automatically bound by the code rights granted by O, but can be bound if the telecoms operator takes appropriate action. As set out in Chapter 3, Paragraphs 10(4) and 20(1)(b) Code provide that a telecoms operator can, after O has granted code rights to it, serve a Paragraph 20 notice on *"any other*

[2] Ibid, Paragraph 10(2).

[3] Ibid, Paragraph 10(3).

person with an interest in the land",[4] where the said land is already subject to *"a code right which is exercisable by the operator"*.[5]

So, where O is the lessee of a piece of land, the freeholder (and any intermediate landlords) are not bound by the code rights conferred by O unless and until they:

(1) Agree to be bound by them; or

(2) Are compelled to agree to be bound by them by the court, following service of a Paragraph 20 notice on them.

The former, simple agreement to be bound, is the means by which the first applicant code operator in *EE Ltd and Hutchison 3G UK Ltd v Edelwind Ltd and the Secretary of State for Housing, Communities and Local Government* [6] bound the freeholder to the code rights granted to it by the second respondent freeholder. The latter, compulsion under Paragraph 20, is the method which Lewison LJ suggested that Cornerstone bind Compton to code rights granted by Vodafone to Cornerstone in *Cornerstone Telecommunications Infrastructure Ltd v Compton Beauchamp Estates Ltd* at [89].[7]

Once a third party has been bound by code rights pursuant to Paragraph 10(4) of the Code, there is a third class of third parties who also become automatically bound by the code rights granted by O, which are set out in Paragraph 10(5):

"If such a person ("P") agrees to be bound by the code right, the code right also binds—

(a) the successors in title to P's interest,

---

[4] Ibid, Paragraph 20(1)(b).

[5] Ibid, Paragraph 10(4).

[6] [2020] UKUT 272 (LC), considered in more detail in Chapter 8.

[7] [2019] EWCA Civ 1755, considered in more detail in Chapter 3.

(b) a person with an interest in the land that is created after P agrees to be bound and is derived (directly or indirectly) out of—

(i) P's interest, or

(ii) the interest of a successor in title to P's interest, and

(c) any other person at any time in occupation of the land whose right to occupation was granted by—

(i) P, at a time when P was bound by the code right, or

(ii) a person within paragraph (a) or (b)."[8]

And in respect of successors in title bound by a code right under Paragraph 10(5)(a), they are *"to be treated as a party to the agreement by which P agreed to be bound by the right."*[9]

So, where P is the freeholder of the land in question and O was P's direct lessee:

(1) P's (for example) assigns will be bound, and will be treated as a party to P's agreement to be bound by the same code rights that O conferred;

(2) If P (or P's assigns) grant an intermediate lease of the land to a third party, superior to O's lease, that lessee will be bound; and

(3) If P (or P's assigns) grant a licence to occupy the land to a third party, after the expiry of O's lease, that licensee will be bound.[10]

---

[8] Communications Act 2003, Schedule 3A, Paragraph 10(5).

[9] Ibid, Paragraph 10(6).

[10] P's agreement with the code operator to be bound by the code rights conferred by O will be a freestanding code agreement that will remain enforceable even after O's code agreement with the code operator is no longer enforceable against O (e.g. because O's interest in the land has extinguished and/or O's occupation of the land has ended).

The Land Registration Act 2002

Usually, whether rights over registered land bind third parties is dictated by the workings of the 2002 Act. However, in respect of the Code, Paragraph 14 provides as follows:

"Where an enactment requires interests, charges or other obligations affecting land to be registered, the provisions of this code about who is bound by a code right have effect whether or not that right is registered."

So, code rights bind the third parties set out above without the need for them to be registered in accordance with the 2002 Act.[11] But this begs the question of how Parliament's intention that code rights need not be registered interacts is reflected in Paragraph 101 of the Code, which reads:

"The ownership of property does not change merely because the property is installed on or under, or affixed to, any land by any person in exercise of a right conferred by or on accordance with this code."

How the 2002 Act and Paragraphs 14 and 101 interact was decisive to the determination of one issue in dispute in *Cornerstone Telecommunications Infrastructure Ltd v Keast*.[12] In that case, Cornerstone sought to acquire code rights from Mr Keast over a small parcel of land which already had a telephone mast and other equipment installed on it by Vodafone under the Old Code.

Mr Keast argued that Cornerstone was not entitled to the code rights it sought because:

(1) The Code regulates the legal relationship between code operators and occupiers of land;[13]

[11] And the provisions of the Code about who is bound by a code right will simply have effect in respect of unregistered land.

[12] [2019] UKUT 116 (LC).

[13] See e.g. Communications Act 2003, Schedule 3A, Paragraphs 3, 9, 20 and 105, as discussed in Chapters 2 and 3.

(2) Paragraph 108(1) of the Code explains that –

""land" does not include electronic communications apparatus";[14]

(3) The telecoms apparatus installed by Vodafone under the Old Code has become part of the land under the common law principles related to the annexure of chattels to land [15] notwithstanding Paragraph 27(4) of the Old Code, which mirrors Paragraph 101 of the Code –

"The ownership of any property shall not be affected by the fact that it is installed on or under, or affixed to, any land by any person in the exercise of a right conferred by or in accordance with this code";[16]
and so

(4) By seeking code rights over the parcel of land in dispute, Cornerstone was in fact seeking code rights over telecoms apparatus, which is not permitted under the Code.

The first issue for Cooke J to consider was whether Paragraph 27(4) of the Old Code (and by extension Paragraph 101 of the Code):

(1) Merely prevents chattels, when becoming part of the land by annexure upon being affixed to it under the common law, from having their ownership passed from the telecoms operator to the landowner; or

(2) Goes one step further and also disapplies the common law rule that the chattels, upon being fixed to the land, become part of the land.

Cooke J's answer was reached by considering how the Code was intended by Parliament to interact with the 2002 Act. She found that:

"If part of an operator's ECA [(electronic communications apparatus)] *on a mast site were to become land, albeit without a change in ownership, then the Code operator will not be able to sell that part of its apparatus without*

[14] Ibid, Paragraph 108(1).

[15] [2019] UKUT 116 (LC) at [32].

[16] Telecommunications Act 1984, Schedule 2, Paragraph 24(4).

making a transfer by deed in accordance with section 52 of the Law of Property Act 1925, and on sale title to that ECA *would be registrable pursuant to Section 4 of the Land Registration Act 2002. That would be an obviously absurd result and cannot have been part of Parliament' intention."* [17]

Cooke J then determined that Paragraph 101 of the Code operates to disapply the common law rule that would otherwise see telecoms apparatus become land upon being affixed to it. She went on to also find in favour of Cornerstone on the second issue of whether it could acquire code rights over the land in question:

"The prohibition upon the acquisition of Code rights over ECA does not mean that it is impossible to acquire Code rights over land where ECA is present." [18]

So whilst Paragraph 14 of the Code provides that code rights themselves need not be registered under the 2002 Act in order to bind third partes, the whole scheme of the Code is intended to work together to ensure that no parties to code agreements are placed in a position where they are required to comply with any registration requirements prescribed under the 2002 Act in order for their rights, obligations or interests arising under the Code to be binding on third parties.

The Assignment of Code Rights

A code operator's right to assign the benefit of a code agreement that it has acquired from either O or P to another code operator is protected under Paragraph 16 of the Code:[19]

"(1) Any agreement under Part 2 of this code is void to the extent that—

[17] [2019] UKUT 116 (LC) at [44].

[18] Ibid, at [48].

[19] Save that these provisions do not apply where the exercise of the code right conferred under the said code agreement depends on a right that has effect pursuant to an agreement that was entered into under the Old Code. See Chapter 11 and Digital Economy Act 2017, Schedule 2, Paragraph 5(2).

(a) it prevents or limits assignment of the agreement to another operator, or

(b) it makes assignment of the agreement to another operator subject to conditions (including a condition requiring the payment of money)...

(4) From the time when the assignment of an agreement under Part 2 of this code takes effect, the assignee is bound by the terms of the agreement.

(5) The assignor is not liable for any breach of a term of the agreement that occurs after the assignment if (and only if), before the breach took place, the assignor or the assignee gave a notice in writing to the other party to the agreement which—

(a) identified the assignee, and

(b) provided an address for service (for the purposes of Paragraph 91(2)(a)) for the assignee." [20]

Not only does this allow for a market in which competing code operators can freely trade their telecoms apparatus with one another, but it also facilitates code operators setting up joint ventures like Cornerstone. If Vodafone and Telefonica acquire code rights under the Code themselves, then they can subsequently agree to transfer the governing code agreements to Cornerstone for joint management of those rights without fear of this potentially uneconomical owing to the need to comply with potentially onerous conditions before being able to do so.

There is one condition, however, which is permitted:

"(2) Sub-paragraph (1) does not apply to a term that requires the assignor to enter into a guarantee agreement...

(6) Sub-paragraph (5) is subject to the terms of any guarantee agreement.

(7) A "guarantee agreement" is an agreement, in connection with the assignment of an agreement under Part 2 of this code, under which the assignor guarantees to any extent the performance by the assignee of the

[20] Communications Act 2003, Schedule 3A, Paragraph 16(1), (4) and (5).

obligations that become binding on the assignee under sub-paragraph (4) (the "relevant obligations").

(8) An agreement is not a guarantee agreement to the extent that it purports—

(a) to impose on the assignor a requirement to guarantee in any way the performance of the relevant obligations by a person other than the assignee, or

(b) to impose on the assignor any liability, restriction or other requirement of any kind in relation to a time after the relevant obligations cease to be binding on the assignee.

(9) Subject to sub-paragraph (8), a guarantee agreement may—

(a) impose on the assignor any liability as sole or principal debtor in respect of the relevant obligations;

(b) impose on the assignor liabilities as guarantor in respect of the assignee's performance of the relevant obligations which are no more onerous than those to which the assignor would be subject in the event of the assignor being liable as sole or principal debtor in respect of any relevant obligation;

(c) make provision incidental or supplementary to any provision within paragraph (a) or (b)."[21]

This form of guarantee, stronger than merely being made surety, substantially mirrors the kind of guarantee that can be imposed under an authorised guarantee agreement under Section 16 of the Landlord and Tenant (Covenants) Act 1995. This guarantee should be some comfort to O or P, provided that they remember to insist that any code agreement that they enter into with a code operator includes the entry into of such a guarantee on any assignment (if this is not freely offered by the code operator in its Paragraph 20 notice).

[21] Ibid, Paragraph 16(2), and (6) to (9).

Summary

In summary:

(1) There are three classes of third parties that can be bound by code agreements. The first is bound automatically, and includes assigns of, and those deriving interests or occupation from, the occupier. The second is bound only upon free agreement, or agreement being imposed by the court after service of a Paragraph 20 notice, and includes all those with an interest in the land in question. The third is bound automatically too, and includes the assigns of, and those deriving interests or occupation from, an individual from the second class that has become bound;

(2) Code rights, whilst being rights that affect land, do not need to be registered under the 2002 Act. The Code is designed to ensure that code rights bind third parties unimpeded by registration rules; and

(3) A code operator's right to assign their end of a code agreement is protected from any conditions under Paragraph 16 of the Code, save that code agreements can require that code operators provide a guarantee in respect of the obligations being taken on by their assign.

CHAPTER TWELVE

THE TRANSITIONAL PROVISIONS

In this penultimate chapter we consider the transitional provisions between the Old Code and the Code set out in Schedule 2 of the Digital Economy Act 2017 ("**the transitional provisions**"), in particular:

(1) What are referred to in the transitional provisions as subsisting agreements; and

(2) The extent to which parts of the Old Code and the Code apply to subsisting agreements.

We do not consider the operation of the Old Code in any detail, as that lies outside the scope of this book. For those reading this chapter looking to understand to what extent the Code may apply to an agreement under the Old Code, we therefore assume the reader is sufficiently familiar with the relevant provisions of the Old Code.

Subsisting Agreements

The starting point in understanding the transitional provisions is to identify what it refers to as subsisting agreements, which are defined in Paragraph 1(4) of those provisions:

"A "subsisting agreement" means–

(a) an agreement for the purposes of paragraph 2 or 3 of the [Old Code]*, or*

(b) an order under paragraph 5 of the existing code,

which is in force, as between an operator and any person, at the time the new code comes into force (and whose terms do not provide for it to cease to have effect at that time)."

And the time the Code came into force was 28 December 2017.

Subsisting agreements have effect from 28 December 2017 *"as an agreement under Part 2 of the new code between the same parties, subject to the modifications made by this Schedule."* [1] Similarly, *"A person who is bound by a right by virtue of paragraph 2(4) of the* [Old Code] *is, after the new code comes into force, treated as bound pursuant to Part 2 of the new code."*[2] The fact that subsisting agreements are treated as code agreements under Part 2 of the Code is key, given that (as set out in Chapter 8) Part 5 of the Code applies to code agreements under Part 2. This is discussed in more detail below.

The Parts of Each the Old Code and Code that Apply to Subsisting Agreements

Whilst the Old Code has not been in force as a whole since 28 December 2017, the Code does not simply apply retrospectively to all subsisting agreements. The transitional provisions keep some parts of the Old Code in force as long as subsisting agreements exist.[3]

Code Rights and Persons Bound by Them

Notwithstanding that the Old Code is no longer in force, people remain bound by subsisting agreements:

"(1) A person bound by a code right by virtue only of paragraph 2(3) of the [Old Code] *continues to be bound by it so long as they would be bound if paragraph 2(3) of the* [Old Code] *continued to have effect.*

(2) In relation to such a person, paragraph 4(4) to (12) of the [Old Code] *continue to have effect, but as if in paragraph 4(4)(b) the reference to*

[1] Digital Economy Act 2017, Schedule 2, Paragraph 2(1).

[2] Ibid, Paragraph 2(2).

[3] Once the last subsisting agreement has come to an end, the Old Code will become entirely obsolete by virtue of it no longer being possible to enter into agreements under the Old Code and there being no subsisting agreements left to which any part of it is preserved to apply under the transitional provisions.

paragraph 21 of the [Old Code] *were a reference to Part 6 of the new code."* [4]

So, the provisions under the Old Code in respect of rights to require the removal of telecoms apparatus do not apply to subsisting agreements. Part 6 of the Code applies to them instead. [5]

In respect of subsisting agreements, to the extent that parts of the Code (like Part 6) apply to them, references in the Code to a code right are:

"(a) in relation to the operator and the land to which an agreement for the purposes of paragraph 2 of the [Old Code] *relates, references to a right for the statutory purposes to do the things listed in paragraph 2(1)(a) to (c) of the* [Old Code]*;*

(b) in relation to land to which an agreement for the purposes of paragraph 3 of the [Old Code] *relates, a right to do the things mentioned in that paragraph."* [6]

<u>Assignment of Code Rights, and Upgrading and Sharing of Apparatus</u>

Pursuant to Paragraph 5 of the transitional provisions:

"(1) Part 3 of the new code (assignment of code rights, and upgrading and sharing of apparatus) does not apply in relation to a subsisting agreement.

(2) Part 3 of the new code does not apply in relation to a code right conferred under the new code if, at the time when it is conferred, the exercise of the right depends on a right that has effect under a subsisting agreement."

So not only does Part 3 of the Code not apply to subsisting agreements, it also does not apply to agreements entered into under the Code if the code rights conferred thereunder depend on code rights enjoyed under a separate subsisting agreement to be exercised.

---

[4] Digital Economy Act 2017, Schedule 2, Paragraph 4.

[5] For which, see Chapter 10.

[6] Digital Economy Act 2017, Schedule 2, Paragraph 3.

Notices Given under the Transitional Provisions

Pursuant to Paragraph 23 of the transitional provisions, any notices given under the transitional provisions have their content and rules for service governed by Part 15 of the Code.[7]

Notices and Applications for Code Rights under the Old Code

Paragraphs 11 of the transitional provisions provides that notices given before 28 December 2017 in order to acquire code rights under the Old Code will be treated as Paragraph 20 notices on any application made after that date. However, pursuant to Paragraph 12, where the application is also made before 28 December 2017, the application will be resolved under the Old Code but take effect as an order under Paragraph 20 of the Code.

Nearly four years after the coming into force of the Code, it is likely that these paragraphs of the transitional provisions are now obsolete.

Paragraph 13 provides that the coming into force of the Code does not affect *"any application or order made under paragraph 6"* of the Old Code, which relates to applications or orders for temporary rights under the Old Code pending applications for code rights under the Old Code. Similarly, this too is now likely obsolete.

Tree Lopping Notices and Applications under the Old Code

Paragraphs 18 and 19 of the transitional provisions work similarly to Paragraphs 11 and 12, save in respect of tree lopping rather than the acquisition of code rights.

Pursuant to Paragraph 18 of the transitional provisions, where a notice is given before 28 December 2017 under Paragraph 19 of the Old Code it (and any counter-notice given thereunder) will take effect under Paragraph 82 of the Code on any application made after that date.

---

[7] For which see Chapter 3.

However, pursuant to Paragraph 19 of the transitional provisions, where the relevant application is made under the Old Code prior to 28 December 2017, the Old Code will continue to apply to it instead of Paragraph 82 of the Code.

As with Paragraphs 11 and 12 of the transitional provisions, it is likely that Paragraphs 18 and 19 are now obsolete too.

Compensation

Pursuant to Paragraph 14 of the transitional provisions, the repeal of the Old Code does not affect its Paragraph 16 (dictating the circumstances where compensation was payable by a code operator under the Old Code for the exercise by it of code rights) or any other right to compensation in respect only of the exercise of code rights prior to 28 December 2017.

Further, Paragraph 25 of the transitional provisions provides that, in order to avoid double recovery:

"A person entitled to compensation by virtue of this Schedule is not entitled to compensation in respect of the same matter under any provision of the new code".

These provisions will become obsolete once the relevant limitation period for such compensation claims has expired, if they have not become so already by virtue of there being no extant potential claims under Paragraph 16 of the Old Code (through Paragraph 14 of the transitional provisions) remaining.

Continuation, Termination and Modification of Subsisting Agreements

Paragraphs 6 of the transitional provisions is, practically speaking, likely the most significant provision contained therein.

First, recall that subsisting agreements now take effect as an agreement under Part 2 of the Code.[8] Second, that Part 5 of the Code applies to all

[8] Digital Economy Act 2017, Schedule 2, Paragraph 2.

agreements under Part 2 of the Code, subject to Paragraphs 29(2) to (4) of the Code.[9]

Pursuant to Paragraph 6(1) of the transitional provisions:

"This paragraph applies in relation to a subsisting agreement, in place of paragraph 29(2) to (4) of the new code."

Paragraphs 6(2) and (3) [10] of the transitional provisions set out that Part 5 of the Code does not apply to a lease of land in England and Wales if it is one to which Part 2 of the 1954 Act:[11]

(1) Applies, granting security of tenure for business, professional and other tenants;[12] or

(2) Does not apply, only and so does not confer security of tenure, but only by virtue of an agreement to exclude that security entered into pursuant to Section 38A of the 1954 Act *and* the primary purpose of the lease is not to grant code rights (within the meaning of Paragraph 3 of the transitional provisions).[13]

Those with a keen eye and good memory will have noticed that these replacement provisions apply slightly differently to Paragraphs 29(2) and (3) of the Code,[14] in that Part 5 of the Code does not apply to:

(1) Code agreements entered into under the Code with security of tenure under Part 2 of the 1954 Act whose primary purpose is not to grant code rights;

[9] Communications Act 2003, Schedule 3A, Paragraph 29(1). See Chapter 8 for code agreements that are not subsisting agreements.

[10] Paragraph 6(4) of the transitional provisions is not considered here as it relates only to leases of land in Northern Ireland.

[11] Landlord and Tenant Act 1954.

[12] Digital Economy Act 2017, Schedule 2, Paragraph 6(2).

[13] Ibid, Paragraph 6(3).

[14] For which, see Chapter 8.

(2) Subsisting agreements that are leases with security of tenure under Part 2 of the 1954 Act; and

(3) Both Code agreements entered into under the Code and subsisting agreements, which are leases with security of tenure under Part 2 of the 1954 Act excluded under Section 38A, and whose primary purpose is not to grant code rights.

The difference being that if a subsisting agreement has security of tenure under Part 2 of the 1954 Act, it does not matter whether its primary purpose is or is not to grant code rights under the Old Code; Part 5 of the Code will not apply to it. The same may not be said for code agreements entered into under the Code that enjoy security of tenure under Part 2 of the 1954 Act; whether or not Part 5 of the Code applies will depend entirely on the primary purpose of the agreement.[15]

The application of Paragraph 6 of the transitional provisions was an issue in dispute in *Cornerstone Telecommunications Infrastructure Ltd v Ashloch Ltd and AP Wireless II (UK) Ltd*.[16] In that case:

(1) Ashloch Ltd ("**Ashloch**") owned the freehold of a rooftop site. Part of the site was subject to an agreement between Vodafone and the previous owner ("**the Tenancy**");

(2) The Tenancy was for the installation of telecoms apparatus on the site, and enjoyed with security of tenure under Part II of the 1954 Act. Its contractual term expired in 2012, but Vodafone remained in occupation of the site thereafter;

(3) In October 2018, AP Wireless II (UK) Ltd ("**APW**") (a company that specialised in the acquisition of leasehold telecoms sites) took a ninety-nine-year lease of the rooftop site from Ashloch;

---

[15] But it is not possible for code agreements entered into under the Code in the form a lease to enjoy both the benefit of Part 5 of the Code and security of tenure under Part 2 of the 1954 Act, by virtue of Section 43(4) of the 1954 Act. For those code agreements, security of tenure under Part 2 of the 1954 Act is excluded. See Chapter 8.

[16] [2021] EWCA Civ 90.

(4) On a date after the decision of the Court of Appeal in *Cornerstone Telecommunications Infrastructure Ltd v Compton Beauchamp Estates Ltd*,[17] Vodafone assigned the Tenancy to Cornerstone;

(5) Cornerstone then served APW with a Paragraph 20 notice, requiring it to enter into a new code agreement. Cornerstone did to because it considered that it was more advantageous to require APW to enter into a new agreement under the Code than to seek a new lease under Part 2 of the 1954 Act; and

(6) APW argued that, in the light of the decision of the Court of Appeal in *Compton Beauchamp*, Cornerstone was in fact the occupier of the site, and as a result could not make use of Paragraph 20 of the Code to acquire a code agreement from APW. APW argued that Cornerstone's sole means of acquiring new rights over the site was under Part 2 of the 1954 Act.

The Court of Appeal followed its decision in *Compton Beauchamp* that the primary test of occupation was one of fact rather than legal status, and determined that Cornerstone was indeed the occupier of the site and so could not apply under Paragraph 20 of the Code.

The Court of Appeal went on to clarify that the Tenancy, being a subsisting agreement to which Part 2 of the 1954 Act applies, was not one to which Part 5 of the Code applies under the transitional provisions (so Cornerstone could not acquire a new code agreement from APW e.g. through variation of the Tenancy by novation under Paragraph 33 of the Code). Instead, Cornerstone's sole means of acquiring new rights over the site was indeed under Part 2 of the 1954 Act, as argued by APW.

So the Court of Appeal upheld the decision of the Tribunal (which was described by Lewison LJ as "*careful, detailed and impressive*" [18]) and dismissed the appeal.

Lewison LJ's judgment in *Ashloch* contains a detailed and fascinating analysis of the Code. We recommend in particular his judgment at [7]-

---

[17] [2019] EWCA Civ 1755, considered in detail in Chapter 3.

[18] [2021] EWCA Civ 90 at [2].

[46] (which gives a detailed explanation of the origins of the Old Code and the nature of the Code) and [86]-[105] (where he takes the time to break down and consider the parts of the transitional provisions, in particular the circumstances in which code operators are able to renew their code agreements under the Code or the 1954 Act).

Further insight was given into the intended workings of Part 5 of the Code in the context of subsisting agreements in *EE Ltd and Hutchison 3G UK Ltd v Stephenson and AP Wireless (II) UK Ltd*.[19] Mr Justice Fancourt noted at [30] that whist Paragraph 30 of the Code provides for code rights to continue, where the agreement is a subsisting agreement this *"can reasonably be seen as a temporary position… rather than the basis for a continuing relationship."* The core reason for this being that where code rights under the new scheme of the Code are available to the code operator *"the prolonged continuation of pre-Code rights is not a satisfactory substitute for a new agreement, at least from an operator's perspective."*

Paragraph 7 of the transitional provisions then goes on to provide a few ways in which Part 5 applies differently to subsisting agreements:

"(2) The "site provider" (see paragraph 30(1)(a) of the new code) does not include a person who was under the [Old Code] *bound by the agreement only by virtue of paragraph 2(2)(c) of that code.*

(3) Where the unexpired term of the subsisting agreement at the coming into force of the new code is less than 18 months, paragraph 31 [of the Code] *applies (with necessary modification) as if for the period of 18 months referred to in sub-paragraph 3(a) there were substituted a period equal to the unexpired term or 3 months, whichever is greater."*

(4) Paragraph 34 applies with the omission of sub-paragraph (13)(d)."

So Paragraph 7(3) relaxes the date requirements in Paragraph 31 of the Code for subsisting agreements with short unexpired terms.[20] Perhaps more importantly, Paragraph 7(4) of the transitional provisions is

[19] [2021] UKUT 167 (LC). See Chapter 9 for a summary of the relevant facts.

[20] See Chapter 8 for consideration of the date requirements of code agreements that are not subsisting agreements.

designed to prevent the Tribunal, when considering what order to make under Paragraph 34 of the Code, from taking into account the consideration payable under an agreement whose consideration was fixed under the valuation principles contained in the Old Code, thereby preserving the sanctity of the new valuation principles set out in the Code.[21]

Objections to and Removal of Apparatus

Paragraph 15 of the transitional provisions provides that:

"The repeal of the [Old Code] *does not affect paragraphs 17 and 18 of that code as they apply in relation to anything whose installation was completed before the repeal comes into force."*

Paragraphs 17 and 18 of the Old Code relate to the site provider's ability to object to the installation of telecoms apparatus installed wholly or partly 3 metres or more above the ground, and the code operator's duty to fix appropriate notices to said apparatus.

Paragraph 16 of the transitional provisions goes on to provide that the repeal of the Old Code does not affect Paragraph 20 of the Old Code (under which, *inter alia*, any person with an interest in the land or neighbouring land could give notice requiring the removal of telecoms apparatus *"on the ground that the alteration is necessary to enable that person to carry out a proposed improvement of the land in which he has an interest"*) [22] as it applies in relation to telecoms apparatus whose installation was completed before 28 December 2017.[23]

However, pursuant to Paragraph 16(2) and (3) of the transitional provisions:

"(2) A right under paragraph 20 [of the Old Code] *is not by virtue of sub-paragraph (1) exercisable in relation to any apparatus by a person who is*

[21] For which, see Chapter 6.

[22] Telecommunications Act 1984, Schedule 2, Paragraph 20(1) as in force on 27 December 2017.

[23] Digital Economy Act 2017, Schedule 2, Paragraph 16(1).

a party to, or is bound by, an agreement under the new code in relation to the apparatus.

(3) A subsisting agreement is not an agreement under the new code for the purposes of sub-paragraph (2)."

So, pursuant to Paragraphs 15 to 17 of the transitional provisions, where telecoms apparatus is fully installed on land pursuant to the Old Code prior to 28 December 2017, the provisions of the Old Code in relating to objection to or removal of that apparatus will apply. The sole exception is that the Old Code's removal for redevelopment provisions will not apply where the relevant apparatus has since become subject to a code right under the Code.

In return for these provisions applying to telecoms apparatus installed prior to 28 December 2017, Paragraph 17 of the transitional provisions dictates that:

"Part 12 of the new code does not apply in relation to apparatus whose installation was completed before the new code came into force."[24]

Separately, pursuant to Paragraph 20 of the transitional provisions, where prior to 28 December 2017 a notice was given under Paragraph 21(2) of the Old Code requiring the removal of apparatus as of right:

"(2) The repeal does not affect the operation of paragraph 21 in relation to anything done or that may be done under that paragraph following the giving of the notice.

(3) For the purposes of applying that paragraph after the repeal comes into force, steps specified in a counter- notice under sub-paragraph 4(b) of that paragraph as steps which the operator proposes to take under the existing code are to be read as including any corresponding steps that the operator could take under the new code or by virtue of this Schedule."

[24] The application of Part 12 of the Code falls outside the scope of this book.

However, as it is likely that no such notices given prior to 28 December 2017 remain unresolved, it is very likely that Paragraph 20 of the transitional provisions is now obsolete.

Parts 7 to 11 of the Code

Paragraphs 8 to 10 and 21 of the transitional provisions make provision in respect of those parts of the Old Code that correspond broadly to Parts 7 to 11 of the Code, which lie outside the scope of this book.

Summary

In summary:

(1) The transitional provisions deal with the parts of the Old Code and the Code that apply to subsisting agreements i.e. agreements entered into under the Old Code before 28 December 2018 whose term does not cease upon the coming into force of the Code;

(2) Persons bound by subsisting agreements continue to be bound by them notwithstanding the repeal of the Old Code;

(3) Whereas Part 3 of the Code does not apply to subsisting agreements, Part 6 does;

(4) Any notices given under the transitional provisions must comply with Part 15 of the Code;

(5) For the most part, notices given under the Old Code prior to 28 December 2017 take effect under their equivalent provision in the Code thereafter, but these provisions are now likely obsolete by virtue of nearly four years having passed since that date;

(6) Compensation payable for use of code rights prior to 28 December 2017 remains governed by the Old Code's valuation principles;

(7) Whether a code operator is able to renew their subsisting agreement under the Code or Part 2 of the 1954 Act was put most pithily by Lewison LJ in *Ashloch* at [98] –

> *"In general where an operator holds under an existing written agreement, it is entitled to apply to renew that agreement under Part 5 of the Code. The only express exception is where the operator holds under*

a lease which entitles it to apply to renew under Part II of the 1954 Act. If the primary purpose of the lease was to grant Code rights, then after the first renewal, the new lease will fall within the scope of Part 5 of the Code. If it was not, then the new lease will remain outside the scope of Part 5 of the Code. Thus one way or another the operator under a subsisting agreement has the right to apply to renew it, either under Part 5 of the Code or under Part II of the Landlord and Tenant Act 1954."
; and

(8) Part 12 of the Code does not apply to subsisting agreements. Instead, provision is made for various rights to object to or require the removal of apparatus under the Old Code to be preserved in respect of apparatus fully installed before 28 December 2017.

CHAPTER THIRTEEN

ADR, PROCEDURES AND PRACTICALITIES

In this final chapter we consider:

(1) Pre-action engagement and ADR;

(2) How to commence proceedings;

(3) The response to proceedings;

(4) Statements of case;

(5) The timetable for determining applications;

(6) Directions;

(7) Evidence and hearings; and

(8) Costs

Pre-action Engagement and ADR

At the end of the T371 Notice of Reference, which a the form used in the Tribunal for cases including applications under the Code, there are notes entitled *"Guidance on Case Management Procedures"*. These notes include the following:

"***Alternative Dispute Resolution/Mediation***

The Tribunal supports the resolution of disputes by agreement between the parties. Information about mediation services ... is available on our website or may be requested from the Tribunal. The Tribunal will usually delay determination of the reference where the parties wish to attempt mediation or other form of ADR."

Further, in the Practice Note [1] the Honourable Mr Justice Holgate referred to the requirement that the Tribunal resolve the dispute within six months and considered "*In view of this requirement pre-action engagement between the parties is strongly encouraged.*" The Upper Tribunal Guidance clearly applies to applications under the Code, but it is anticipated that the Tribunal will be anxious to avoid delay in view of the tight and inflexible timetable and so the parties to a dispute should indeed, endeavour to engage in ADR prior to the issue of proceedings if at all possible.

Disputes under the Code are well suited to mediation. The flexibility of mediation enables a practical approach to dispute resolution which can avoid the need for proceedings. There are a number of specialist property mediators able to assist with these cases.

Other forms of ADR may also be used.

The Commencement of Proceedings

The procedure for commencing proceedings is governed by Part 5 of the Rules,[2] and as set out above the relevant form is the T371 Notice of Reference. Rule 28 provides as follows:

"(1) Proceedings to which this Part applies must be started by way of reference made by sending or delivering to the Tribunal a notice of reference.

(2) The parties to the proceedings are the person making the reference and any person named as a party in the notice of reference.

(3) The notice of reference must be signed and dated and must state—

(a) the name and address of the person making the reference and, if represented,—

(i) the name and address of that person's representative; and

(ii) the professional capacity, if any, in which the person's representative acts;

[1] Practice Note: Electronic Communications Code.

[2] Tribunal Procedure (Upper Tribunal) (Lands Chamber) Rules 2010, as amended.

(b) an address where documents for the person making the reference may be sent or delivered;

(bb) the name and address of any person named as a party other than the person making the reference;

(c) the address or description of the land to which the reference relates;

(d) the name and address of every other person—

(i) with an interest in the land or property; or (ii) in occupation of the land or property;

(e) the nature of the—

(i) interest in the land or property; and

(ii) the right of occupation;

(f) the statutory provision under which the reference is made (unless the reference is a reference by consent under section 1(5) of the 1949 Act);

(g) if the reference is made by a claimant for compensation or other monetary award, the amount claimed, an explanation of how that amount is calculated and a summary of the reasons for making that claim;

(h) the matter on which the person making the reference seeks the determination of the Tribunal and a summary of the reasons for seeking that determination and, where the reference is an appeal under the Riot Compensation Act 2016, the grounds of appeal on which the applicant relies; and

(i) whether the person making the reference wants the reference to be determined without a hearing."

Form T371 contains those matters required under the Rules, including details of the person making the reference, of any representative, of the capacity of the person making the reference, and the form provides for a tick box choice (in so far as material to applications under the Code) between "*land owner/occupier; Electronic Communications Code operator; or other.*" The Respondent's details and the details of their representative are required.

The Property to which the reference relates must be identified, including a description of the nature of the land (dwelling house, shop, vacant land etc.), the approximate area (if relevant) and the postal address. The statutory provision or agreement giving the right to refer the matter to the Tribunal must be identified, and in cases under the Code confirmation that the claim is under the Code. Details of every other person with an interest in the land, if known must be included.

The form requires information about arrangements for the hearing to be provided. The applicant is required to indicate whether it intends to call an expert witness, or more than one expert witness, although it is permissible to tick the box *"Unsure"*.

The applicant is required to confirm that the attached guidance has been read and to select between:

(1) The standard procedure (used in a case where a hearing is necessary and another procedure is not considered more appropriate);

(2) The special procedure (for cases of greater complexity, value or general importance or where there is another good reason for closer supervision of the Tribunal);

(3) The simplified procedure (for speedy and economical determination of cases in which there is no substantial issue of law or valuation practice and no substantial conflict of fact is likely to arise; and

(4) The written representations procedure (in which cases the Tribunal may direct that the reference will be determined without an oral hearing but will not usually do so without the consent of the parties.

In the event that the applicant has selected any option other than the standard procedure it is necessary to explain why the procedure selected is most suitable.

The Rules provide for certain material to be provided with the notice of reference. As set out at Rule 28(4)(a), a copy of the order or other documents in consequence of which the reference is made including any agreement conferring jurisdiction on the Tribunal. The form has a checklist for enclosures which is to be completed by the applicant.

Rule 28(4)(c) requires the person making the reference to provide the fee. The reference filing fee is £275 at the time of writing. The Tribunal's fees are available on its website, and the fees are as prescribed in the Upper Tribunal (Lands Chamber) Fees (Amendment) Order 2016 (SI 2016/434).

Rule 28(5) provides that the person making the reference must provide sufficient copies for every other person named as a party in the notice of reference of the notice of reference and documents listed in Rule 28(4).

Rule 28(8) requires the Tribunal to send copies of the notice and accompanying documents to the person named in the notice.

The reference and documents can be submitted and tracked digitally online with the E-Filing service https://www.gov.uk/guidance/hmcts-e-filing-service-for-citizens-and-professionals or sent to:

Upper Tribunal (Lands Chamber)
5th Floor
Rolls Building
Fetter Lane
London
EC4A 1NL

DX: 160042 Strand 4

Email: Lands@justice.gov.uk

Tel: 020 7612 9710 Fax: 0870 761 7751

The Response to Notice of Reference

Rule 29(1) requires the person to whom the Tribunal sends a copy of the notice of reference to, within one month of the Tribunal sending the notice, send or deliver to the Tribunal and the party who made the notice of reference a response.

Pursuant to Rule 29(2), the notice must be signed and dated and state whether the person making the response intends to take part in the proceedings. Information is also required including: the name address of the person and of their representative; the professional capacity of the representative; and an address for service of documents. The respondent must also provide a summary of their contentions,[3] and if the respondent is a claimant and the claim is for compensation or a monetary award, the amount claimed, an explanation of how that amount is calculated and a summary of the reasons for making that claim.[4] The respondent is also required to state whether the person wants the reference to be determined without a hearing.[5]

Statements of Case

By Rule 29(3), after receipt of a response to a notice of reference the Tribunal must direct either that the parties must file and serve a statement of case or that the notice of reference and response to a notice of reference shall stand as the statement of case.

The Timetable for Determining Applications

Paragraph 97 of the Code refers to Regulation 3 of the Electronic Communications and Wireless Telegraphy Regulations 2011 ("**the 2011 Regulations**") and records that this makes provision about the time within which certain applications to the court under the Code must be determined.

Regulation 3(2) of the 2011 Regulations require the Tribunal to determine applications for the grant of code rights within six months of receipt of the application. In the interim hearing in *EE Ltd and Hutchinson 3G Ltd v London Borough of Islington* [6] the Tribunal described the requirement for the Tribunal to determine such applications within six months as an "*important feature of the Code... to resolve dispute without delay.*" [7]

In the substantive hearing in *London Borough of Islington* [8] Martin Rodger QC commented at [18]:

---

[3] Rule 29(2)(c).

[4] Rule 29(2)(d)

[5] Rule 29(2)(e)

[6] [2018] UKUT 362 (LC)

[7] Ibid, at [10].

[8] [2019] UKUT 53 (LC)

"...That obligation is imposed in the public interest and is not one which either the parties or the Tribunal are free to dispense with. The Tribunal has interpreted the obligation as applying only to the acquisition of rights over new sites, and not to the renewal of rights over existing sites..."

Directions

Directions are likely to be given at an early stage in cases under the Code, particularly if interim relief is sought. The Practice Note [9] sets out that the first case management hearing in a dispute under the Code is likely to take place within two to three weeks of receipt of the notice of reference, and will usually be held on a Friday and if more convenient to one or both of the parties may be by telephone. In *EE Ltd and Hutchinson 3G Ltd v London Borough of Islington*,[10] the interim rights proceedings in that case, Martin Rodger QC gave directions on the day the application was issued.

The Upper Tribunal Guidance on Case Management Procedures provides a warning about compliance with directions as follows:

"***All cases – compliance with directions***

Parties are expected to comply with a direction that has been given during the course of proceedings and non-compliance may result in a sanction being imposed. If you are unable to comply with a direction you must make an application promptly for an extension of time or for other variation of the direction(s) before the time for compliance has expired. See Rule 6 for full details of the interlocutory application procedure. You should seek the prior agreement of the other parties and, if it is not given, tell them that any objection must be made in writing to the Tribunal within 10 days. To make an application you must set out your reasons, confirm that you have given notice of the application to all other parties and enclose the fee for an interlocutory application. The fee is £110. Please note that all cheques must be made payable to 'HM Courts & Tribunals Service' (not the Lands Chamber)."

---

[9] Practice Note: Electronic Communications Code.

[10] [2018] UKUT 362 (LC)

As recorded in *London Borough of Islington* [11] at [15], by an order made on 22 October 2018 the Tribunal gave directions for the final determination. The code operator was required to provide an electronic draft of the agreement they sought and the relevant person was directed to return the draft showing any proposed amendments clearly marked on it. The code operator was then to respond to the amendments identifying those which were agreed or disputed. Finally, the parties were required to discuss the draft on a without prejudice basis with a view to narrowing the issues between them before filing the agreement in its final iteration together with a joint statement of the reasons for any remaining points of contention by 19 November 2018. The timetable was agreed. It should be noted that this requirement is likely to be included in most directions orders made by the Tribunal.

The respondent did not comply with the directions and relied upon a witness statement of its expert that explained in a narrative form the areas of disagreement. At [17] of his judgment Martin Rodger QC considered that the "*respondent's disregard of the Tribunal's direction was deliberate*".

The Deputy President referred to the time limit imposed on the Tribunal in such cases and continued at [19]-[21]:

"*The imposition of a time limit for the determination of references under the new Code means that an even higher degree of cooperation with the Tribunal and between the parties is required in these cases. The purpose of the Tribunal's direction for the service and completion of a travelling draft was to facilitate the discharge of its obligation to provide a decision within the 6 months permitted by statute.*

As this case has already demonstrated, the burden on the Tribunal's resources caused by parties who fail to cooperate with each other and with the Tribunal is considerable. The Tribunal had been invited to approach its decision on 19 October 2018 at the level of principle, on the basis that the parties would seek to reach agreement on the detailed drafting of the necessary agreement once it was known whether interim rights were to be imposed. Unfortunately the expectation that a sensible consensus could be achieved over the detailed terms of an interim agreement which was expected to last less than four months proved unjustified. The parties agreed virtually nothing and the

[11] [2019] UKUT 0053.

respondent refused even to allow access for non-invasive surveys while terms remained unresolved. Eventually on 11 December 2018 it was necessary for the Tribunal to settle the form of the agreement, going through the draft document, clause by clause, selecting between the parties' rival formulations.

Before the hearing our expectation had been that part of the two days allotted to it would be devoted to argument on the specific terms of the final agreement which remained in dispute. Without a marked drafts from the respondent, or any document identifying its detailed alternative proposals, it was impossible for that exercise to be undertaken. The respondent appeared instead to anticipate that the Tribunal would resolve issues of principle ... That was not the procedure the Tribunal had directed. Nor was it an acceptable alternative, since the Tribunal is obliged to provide its final decision by 24 February 2019."

The Tribunal rejected the submission of the relevant person that there was an issue of principle to be determined before further drafting could be attempted and continued at [23]-[24]:

"*Where a party fails to co-operate with the Tribunal to such an extent that the Tribunal is unable to deal with the proceedings fairly and justly the Tribunal has power under rule 8(3)(b) of The Tribunal Procedure (Upper Tribunal) (Lands Chamber) Rules 2010 to strike out the whole or part of that party's case. We consider that the respondent's failure in this case falls within that description. The Tribunal cannot force parties to agree, but it can require them clearly to state their case so that it can identify and determine the matters in dispute within the time limit fixed by Parliament.*

For these reasons we indicated at the start of the hearing that the respondent would not be permitted to call evidence or make submissions on the terms of the agreement (as opposed to the consideration and compensation payable). We exempted from that prohibition the issue of principle identified by Mr Wills, namely whether the Code gives the Tribunal power to impose a lease on the parties. As that is a question of jurisdiction it is necessary for the Tribunal to resolve it and it is to that issue which we turn first."

Let this be a cautionary tale to any party in Code proceedings. Serious sanctions will be imposed for non-compliance with directions orders which are made.

Further, there is an obligation upon the parties to co-operate in enabling the Tribunal to meet the strict deadline imposed on it for determining disputes under the Code

Evidence and Hearings

In addition to the case management powers in Rule 5, the Tribunal can give directions as to the issues on which it requires evidence or submissions and the nature of such evidence and submissions by Rule 16. Rule 16 enables the Tribunal to limit the number of witnesses and to direct the manner in which evidence and submissions are given including whether orally or by witness statement or written submissions.

Rule 18 provides that the Tribunal may, on the application of a party or on its own initiative, require any person to attend as a witness and to answer questions or produce documents in that person's possession or control which relate to any issues in the proceedings. If a person is subject to a summons that person may apply to vary or set aside the summons if they did not have an opportunity to object to it before it was made or issued and must do so as soon as reasonably practicable after receipt. A summons must give fourteen days' notice of the hearing or such shorter period as may be directed and, if the person is not a party, make provision for the person's necessary expenses of attendance to be paid and state who is to pay them.

The Tribunal may permit the parties to adduce expert evidence by Rule 16(1)(c). Any such expert evidence must be given in accordance with Rule 17. Pursuant to Rule 17(1), the overriding duty of the expert is to assist the Tribunal with matters within the expert's expertise, and this duty overrides any obligation to the party instructing the expert or by whom the expert is paid. Such expert is to be given by a written report unless the Tribunal directs otherwise.[12] By Rule 17(5) the written report must:

"*(a) contain a statement that the expert understands the duty in paragraph (1) and has complied with it,*

[12] Rule 17(4)

(b) contain the words "I believe that the facts stated in this report are true and that the opinions expressed are correct",

(c) comply with the requirements of any practice direction as regards its form and contents, and

(d) be signed by the expert."

Rule 19 provides that site inspections can be conducted by the Tribunal with the consent of the occupier to inspect land or property which is the subject of the proceedings and as far as practicable any other land or property relevant to the proceedings.

Withdrawal of the proceedings is permitted by and in accordance with Rule 20.

Costs

An award for costs under the Rules relates to the costs of the proceedings and is to be distinguished from consideration and compensation which are considered elsewhere in this book. Rule 10(6)(e) of the Rules provides that the Tribunal has power to award costs in disputes under the Code.[13] Rule 10(1) also empowers the Tribunal to make an order for costs on an application or on its own initiative but only in accordance with Rule 10(3) to (6). This includes:

(1) Its power under Section 29(4) of the Tribunals, Courts and Enforcement Act 2007 (wasted costs) and for incidental costs in applying for an order for such costs;

(2) If the Tribunal considers that a party or its representative has acted unreasonably in bringing, defending or conducting the proceedings; and

[13] This marries with Paragraph 96 of the Code, which gives the Tribunal the power to award costs in code disputes where it exercises jurisdiction pursuant to regulations made under Paragraph 95(1) of the Code (which it does: see Chapter 4 on Regulation 3 of the Electronic Communications Code (Jurisdiction) Regulations 2017).

(3) In the circumstances in Paragraph 10(14) of the Rules, namely to pay the costs of an amount equal to the whole or part of a fee made which is not otherwise included in an award of costs.

Summary

In summary:

(1) Pre-action engagement between the parties is strongly encouraged and mediation is a good forum for disputes about the Code;

(2) Part 5 of the Rules govern how to commence proceedings, and in particular Rule 28 contains requirements which must be met;

(3) A party served with a notice of reference must respond within one month indicating whether it intends to take part in proceedings;

(4) The Tribunal can direct that the parties file and serve statements of case or that the notice of reference and response stand as statements of case;

(5) The timetable for determining applications is six months and there is no power to extend time. In these circumstances, the Tribunal is likely to be even more intolerant to a breach of directions order than would usually be the case;

(6) The Tribunal has broad powers to make directions;

(7) The Tribunal can control evidence at hearings including permitting expert evidence and site visits; and

(8) The Tribunal has power to award costs under its Rules. This is to be distinguished from the power to award payment of consideration or compensation under the Code.

INDEX

MORE BOOKS BY LAW BRIEF PUBLISHING

A selection of our other titles available now:-

'Fundamental Dishonesty and QOCS in Personal Injury Proceedings: Law and Practice' by Jake Rowley
'A Practical Guide to the Law in Relation to School Exclusions' by Charlotte Hadfield & Alice de Coverley
'A Practical Guide to Divorce for the Silver Separators' by Karin Walker
'The Right to be Forgotten – The Law and Practical Issues' by Melissa Stock
'A Practical Guide to Planning Law and Rights of Way in National Parks, the Broads and AONBs' by James Maurici QC, James Neill et al
'A Practical Guide to Election Law' by Tom Tabori
'A Practical Guide to the Law in Relation to Surrogacy' by Andrew Powell
'A Practical Guide to Claims Arising from Fatal Accidents – 2nd Edition' by James Patience
'A Practical Guide to the Ownership of Employee Inventions – From Entitlement to Compensation' by James Tumbridge & Ashley Roughton
'A Practical Guide to Asbestos Claims' by Jonathan Owen & Gareth McAloon
'A Practical Guide to Stamp Duty Land Tax in England and Northern Ireland' by Suzanne O'Hara
'A Practical Guide to the Law of Farming Partnerships' by Philip Whitcomb
'Covid-19, Homeworking and the Law – The Essential Guide to Employment and GDPR Issues' by Forbes Solicitors
'Covid-19, Force Majeure and Frustration of Contracts – The Essential Guide' by Keith Markham
'Covid-19 and Criminal Law – The Essential Guide' by Ramya Nagesh
'Covid-19 and Family Law in England and Wales – The Essential Guide' by Safda Mahmood
'A Practical Guide to the Law of Unlawful Eviction and Harassment – 2nd Edition' by Stephanie Lovegrove
'Covid-19, Residential Property, Equity Release and Enfranchisement – The Essential Guide' by Paul Sams and Louise Uphill
'Covid-19, Brexit and the Law of Commercial Leases – The Essential Guide' by Mark Shelton
'A Practical Guide to Costs in Personal Injury Claims – 2nd Edition' by Matthew Hoe

'A Practical Guide to the General Data Protection Regulation (GDPR) – 2nd Edition' by Keith Markham
'Ellis on Credit Hire – Sixth Edition' by Aidan Ellis & Tim Kevan
'A Practical Guide to Working with Litigants in Person and McKenzie Friends in Family Cases' by Stuart Barlow
'Protecting Unregistered Brands: A Practical Guide to the Law of Passing Off' by Lorna Brazell
'A Practical Guide to Secondary Liability and Joint Enterprise Post-Jogee' by Joanne Cecil & James Mehigan
'A Practical Guide to the Pre-Action RTA Claims Protocol for Personal Injury Lawyers' by Antonia Ford
'A Practical Guide to Neighbour Disputes and the Law' by Alexander Walsh
'A Practical Guide to Forfeiture of Leases' by Mark Shelton
'A Practical Guide to Coercive Control for Legal Practitioners and Victims' by Rachel Horman
'A Practical Guide to Rights Over Airspace and Subsoil' by Daniel Gatty
'Tackling Disclosure in the Criminal Courts – A Practitioner's Guide' by Narita Bahra QC & Don Ramble
'A Practical Guide to the Law of Driverless Cars – Second Edition' by Alex Glassbrook, Emma Northey & Scarlett Milligan
'A Practical Guide to TOLATA Claims' by Greg Williams
'A Practical Guide to Elderly Law – 2nd Edition' by Justin Patten
'A Practical Guide to the Law of Prescription in Scotland' by Andrew Foyle
'A Practical Guide to the Construction and Rectification of Wills and Trust Instruments' by Edward Hewitt
'A Practical Guide to the Law of Bullying and Harassment in the Workplace' by Philip Hyland
'How to Be a Freelance Solicitor: A Practical Guide to the SRA-Regulated Freelance Solicitor Model' by Paul Bennett
'A Practical Guide to Prison Injury Claims' by Malcolm Johnson
'A Practical Guide to the Small Claims Track - 2nd Edition' by Dominic Bright
'A Practical Guide to Advising Clients at the Police Station' by Colin Stephen McKeown-Beaumont

'A Practical Guide to Antisocial Behaviour Injunctions' by Iain Wightwick
'Practical Mediation: A Guide for Mediators, Advocates, Advisers, Lawyers, and Students in Civil, Commercial, Business, Property, Workplace, and Employment Cases' by Jonathan Dingle with John Sephton
'The Mini-Pupillage Workbook' by David Boyle
'A Practical Guide to Crofting Law' by Brian Inkster
'A Practical Guide to Spousal Maintenance' by Liz Cowell
'A Practical Guide to the Law of Domain Names and Cybersquatting' by Andrew Clemson
'A Practical Guide to the Law of Gender Pay Gap Reporting' by Harini Iyengar
'A Practical Guide to the Rights of Grandparents in Children Proceedings' by Stuart Barlow
'NHS Whistleblowing and the Law' by Joseph England
'Employment Law and the Gig Economy' by Nigel Mackay & Annie Powell
'A Practical Guide to Noise Induced Hearing Loss (NIHL) Claims' by Andrew Mckie, Ian Skeate, Gareth McAloon
'An Introduction to Beauty Negligence Claims – A Practical Guide for the Personal Injury Practitioner' by Greg Almond
'Intercompany Agreements for Transfer Pricing Compliance' by Paul Sutton
'Zen and the Art of Mediation' by Martin Plowman
'A Practical Guide to the SRA Principles, Individual and Law Firm Codes of Conduct 2019 – What Every Law Firm Needs to Know' by Paul Bennett
'A Practical Guide to Adoption for Family Lawyers' by Graham Pegg
'A Practical Guide to Industrial Disease Claims' by Andrew Mckie & Ian Skeate
'A Practical Guide to Redundancy' by Philip Hyland
'A Practical Guide to Vicarious Liability' by Mariel Irvine
'A Practical Guide to Applications for Landlord's Consent and Variation of Leases' by Mark Shelton
'A Practical Guide to Relief from Sanctions Post-Mitchell and Denton' by Peter Causton
'A Practical Guide to Equity Release for Advisors' by Paul Sams
'A Practical Guide to Financial Services Claims' by Chris Hegarty

www.ingramcontent.com/pod-product-compliance
Lightning Source LLC
LaVergne TN
LVHW022037200926
848481LV00003B/714